Frommer's™

Sicily
day BY day™

1st Edition

by Adele Evans

WILEY

A John Wiley and Sons, Ltd, Publication

Contents

UK Publisher: Sally Smith
Production Manager: Daniel Mersey
Commissioning Editor: Mark Henshall
Development Editor: Teresa Fisher
Project Editor: Hannah Clement
Photo Research: Jill Emeny
Cartography: John Tulip

Wiley also publishes its books in a variety of electronic formats. Some
content that appears in print may not be available in electronic books.

British Library Cataloguing in Publication Data
A catalogue record for this book is available from the British Library

ISBN: 978-0-470-72118-6

Typeset by Wiley Indianapolis Composition Services
Printed and bound in China by RR Donnelley

5 4 3 2 1

A Note from the Editorial Director

Organizing your time. That's what this guide is all about.

Other guides give you long lists of things to see and do and then expect you to fit the pieces together. The Day by Day guides are different. These guides tell you the best of everything, and then they show you how to see it *in the smartest, most time-efficient way*. Our authors have designed detailed itineraries organized by time, neighborhood, or special interest. And each tour comes with a bulleted map that takes you from stop to stop.

Looking to get close to smouldering Mt. Etna's black lava moonscape, see a show at Taormina's Teatro Greco or swim in the crystalline bays of the Egadi Islands? Planning to marvel at the Roman mosaics of the Villa Romana del Casale, taste wine in the Moorish Marsala or gaze out over the Bay of Taormina at sunset? Whatever your interest or schedule, the Day by Days give you the smartest routes to follow. Not only do we take you to the top attractions, hotels, and restaurants, but we also help you access those special moments that locals get to experience—those "finds" that turn tourists into travelers.

The Day by Days are also your top choice if you're looking for one complete guide for all your travel needs. The best hotels and restaurants for every budget, the greatest shopping values, the wildest nightlife—it's all here.

Why should you trust our judgment? Because our authors personally visit each place they write about. They're an independent lot who say what they think and would never include places they wouldn't recommend to their best friends. They're also open to suggestions from readers. If you'd like to contact them, please send your comments our way at feedback@frommers.com, and we'll pass them on.

Enjoy your Day by Day guide—the most helpful travel companion you can buy. And have the trip of a lifetime.

Warm regards,

Kelly Regan

Kelly Regan, Editorial Director
Frommer's Travel Guides

About the Author

British-born **Adele Evans** is a travel writer and broadcaster who fell in love with Italy at first sight at the age of 12. It was about 10 years later that she made her first trip to the 'little continent'. Ortygia was where she had her 'Eureka' moment, entranced by the sublime melting pot of the Grecian with the Norman, Baroque and beyond with each wave of invaders adding to the cultural—and culinary mix. The delight of savoring snow from Mt Etna with rose-water and jasmine—just as the Arabs did when they invented ice cream, the fusion of flavors set against groves of citrus and olive trees and the perfumed nero d'avola wine draw her back time and time again. For her, this alluring, brooding, mesmerising meeting place of Africa and Europe is like nowhere else on earth. When not globetrotting, Adele returns as often as possible to all places Italian and writes for many national news-papers (from the *Sunday Mirror* to the *Sunday Times*), magazines and web-sites. She is also the author of several guidebooks, especially on Italy and France.

Acknowledgments

Many thanks to my editor Mark Henshall for his gentle nudges, tireless attention and for getting me on board with the book. Grateful thanks, too, to all of the Frommer's team for their most dedicated work. Alessandra, Stefania and Adriana from E.N.I.T. were supremely helpful, friendly and sup-portive—a huge thank you to them and also, very importantly, to Marina Tavolato of Travel Marketing.

Dedication

To my husband, Martin, for his support and endless patience and to vulca-nologist Andrew and lovely Jane. And, not least, to the many Sicilians for sharing their ideas and their glorious island with me.

An Additional Note

Please be advised that travel information is subject to change at any time—and this is especially true of prices. We therefore suggest that you write or call ahead for confirmation when making your travel plans. The authors, edi-tors, and publisher cannot be held responsible for the experiences of read-ers while traveling. Your safety is important to us, however, so we encourage you to stay alert and be aware of your surroundings.

Star Ratings, Icons & Abbreviations

Every hotel, restaurant, and attraction listing in this guide has been ranked for quality, value, service, amenities, and special features using a star-rating system. Hotels, restaurants, attractions, shopping, and nightlife are rated on a scale of zero stars (recommended) to three stars (exceptional). In addition to the star-rating system, we also use a **kids** icon to point out the best bets for families. Within each tour, we recommend cafes, bars, or restaurants where you can take a break. Each of these stops appears in a shaded box marked with a coffee-cup-shaped bullet ☕.

The following **abbreviations** are used for credit cards:

AE	American Express	**DISC**	Discover	**V**	Visa
DC	Diners Club	**MC**	MasterCard		

Travel Resources at Frommer.com

Now that you have this guidebook to help you plan a great trip, visit our website at **www.frommers.com** for additional travel information on more than 4,000 destinations. We update features regularly to give you instant access to the most current trip-planning information available. At Frommers.com, you'll find scoops on the best airfares, lodging rates, and car rental bargains. You can even book your travel online through our reliable travel booking partners.

A Note on Prices

In the "Take a Break" and "Best Bets" sections of this book, we have used a system of dollar signs to show a range of costs for 1 night in a hotel (the price of a double-occupancy room) or the cost of an entree (main course) at a restaurant.

Cost	Hotels	Restaurants
$	under $100	under $10
$$	$100–$200	$10–$20
$$$	$200–$300	$20–$30
$$$$	$300–$400	$30–$40
$$$$$	over $400	over $40

How to Contact Us

In researching this book, we discovered many wonderful places—hotels, restaurants, shops, and more. We're sure you'll find others. Please tell us about them, so we can share the information with your fellow travelers in upcoming editions. If you were disappointed with a recommendation, we'd love to know that, too. Please write to:

Frommer's Sicily Day by Day, 1st Edition
Wiley Publishing, Inc. • 111 River St. • Hoboken, NJ 07030-5774

20 Favorite
Moments

20 Favorite **Moments**

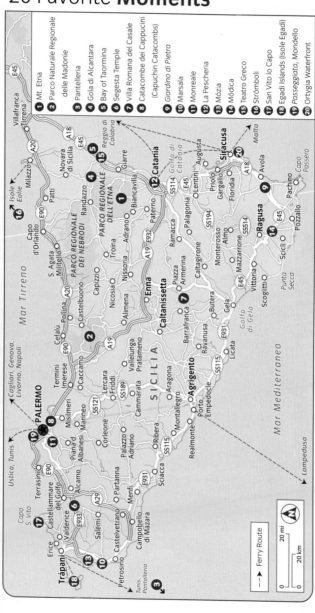

The Mediterranean's largest island is a cradle of civilization. Shaped by its past and the earth-moving volcano Mt. Etna, Sicily has an on-the-brink feel. Since the beginning of human history, every European empire has marched through Sicily, leaving its mark. As the German writer Goethe said: 'To have seen Italy without seeing Sicily is not to have seen Italy at all—for Sicily is the key to everything'.

❶ Get close to Etna—the big Mamma of volcanoes. You'll be aware of the smoldering presence of Europe's largest, highest, and most active volcano everywhere in Sicily, but for jaw-dropping views take the cable car up and walk on the black lava moonscape. You'll feel the heat at your feet, hear the hiss of belching steam, and marvel at the sight of the contrasting green-cloaked mountains and blue waters far below. *See p 30.*

❷ Go wild in the Parco Naturale Regionale delle Madonie. This is Sicily's greatest national park sprawling across 39,679 hectares (98,049 acres). Walk in the traces of wild cats under the beady eye of soaring eagles and marvel at the profusion of wild flowers—including delicate rare orchids and bluest blue *myosotis*. Unforgettable. *See p 36.*

❸ Star-gaze on the castaway island of Pantelleria. Called the Black Pearl of the Mediterranean, you'll be bewitched by the dramatic contrast between the glowering black lava, dazzlingly white-domed 'dammusi' houses, and swimming-pool blue seas. It's the island of choice for celebrities and the floral-shaped capers are the best you'll ever taste. *See p 48.*

❹ Cool off in the Gola di Alcantara. This dramatic gorge carved by the river Alcantara is framed by extraordinary black basalt rock formations. Paddle in protective rubber boots in the icy waters and scramble along the river bed up to the waterfall. *See p 64.*

❺ Gaze out over the Bay of Taormina. Enjoy an *aperitivo* at sunset, looking out from the candlelit roof terrace of the divine Villa Carlotta across the sea in one direction and Mt. Etna in the other—life doesn't get much more blissful than this. *See p 69.*

❻ Discover your favorite temple. Standing alone, high on a hill on the edge of a ravine, the Temple at Segesta is probably the world's most stunningly sited classical monument. It's also one of the most perfect Doric temples ever built, and to see it glow pink at sunrise or sunset is one of Sicily's most romantic visions. *See p 51.*

Get close to Etna.

❼ Marvel at the mosaics of the Villa Romana del Casale. Buried under mud for hundreds of years, excavations began in 1950 to reveal these Roman mosaics of stunning quality and color. Full of life, humor, sensuality—and famously depicting the world's first bikinis—the villa and its treasures are Sicily's most important Roman site. *See p 92.*

❽ Descend into the Catacombe dei Cappucini. Make an appointment with death, Sicilian style. In these catacombs the mummified bodies of 8,000 Palermitans, dressed in their Sunday best, supposedly grin at you. This must be among the world's most macabre sights, and it may sound prurient, but it's an extremely popular attraction—especially with teenagers—but definitely not for the squeamish. *See p 65.*

❾ Stroll through Noto's *Giardino di Pietra.* This 'garden of stone' is of a soft peachy-golden color in, arguably, the most beautiful

Be stunned by the Byzantine mosaics of Monreale.

of Sicily's Baroque towns. *See p 95.*

❿ Taste wine in Marsala. Discover the delights and complexities of this fragrant wine and be amazed by the variations in taste from sweet to spicy and dry. Then meander through the Moorish warren of little streets that are reminiscent of a North African town, where Garibaldi landed with his Thousand in 1860 and started his campaign to make it the first city of a united Italy. *See p 154.*

⓫ Bask in the reflected glory of Monreale. This 12th-century cathedral is smothered in glistening Byzantine mosaics—the world's second largest mosaic-covered surface after Istanbul. A full 2,200kg (4,850 lbs) of pure gold were used in the mosaics that depict stories from the Old and New testaments, created by Byzantine and Arab artisans. Even the cloisters outside, which represent the flowering of Islamic architecture, are often referred to as a 'preview of Paradise'. *See p 57.*

Produce at Catania's famous fish market, La Pescheria.

⑫ **Go fishing in Catania's famous fish market, La Pescheria.** Raw, writhing, and colorful, this is as much a place to immerse yourself in for the full Sicilian experience as it is for the glistening bounty of the sea. In the surrounding alleyways, there's an Aladdin's cave of delights for take-home souvenirs from mounds of aromatic spices to ubiquitous Sicilian carts. *See p 107.*

⑬ **Meander around Mózia.** In the 8th-century BC, this island of the Phoenicians was Italy's most important trading post. Enjoy a picnic among the aloe-fringed paths and ruins in this tranquil spot. *See p 52.*

⑭ **Savor chocolate in Módica.** Traditionally made to an Aztec recipe and famous throughout Italy, Módica's *ciocolatto di vetro* (glass chocolate) combines cocoa and sugar into a crunchy texture flavored with vanilla and cinnamon or spicy peppercorns and chilies. The result is every chocoholic's idea of paradise, as you'll discover by dropping into the mouthwatering

Antica Dolceria Bonajuto, Sicily's oldest chocolate manufacturer. *See p 30.*

⑮ **See a show at Taormina's Teatro Greco.** The setting ticked all the boxes for the Greeks for whom the sea and sky were the natural theatrical backdrop, especially when overseen by a volcano in the shape of Mt. Etna. This originally 3rd-century BC theater is sheer drama of the purest kind. Treat yourself to an open-air performance during the summer festival. *See p 143.*

⑯ **Take a moonlit boat trip around Strómboli.** Even the moonbeams are likely to be eclipsed by the fireworks from the summit of this very active volcano. If you're lucky you may witness 'strombolian' explosions—outbursts of lava ejected high into the air. See glowing red-hot lava as it snakes down the **Sciara del Fuoco** (Slope of Fire), and hear the hiss as it meets the sea. *See p 37.*

⑰ **Sunbathe at San Vito lo Capo.** Go west to the northernmost tip of the island and be immersed in

Taormina's Teatro Greco.

The city-dwellers coastal escape of Mondello.

the soft pinky-white sands that arch along this promontory, backed by jagged cliffs, and fringed by azure seas. You'll be far from alone in high season when Sicilians like their beaches hot and sociable, but off season you could almost have it to yourself. *See p 71.*

⓲ **Swim off the Egadi Islands.** Favignana (also called *La Farfalla* after its 'butterfly' shape) is the largest of the Egadi Islands. The swimming here in crystalline bays is truly spectacular, and there's even a **Grotta degli Innamorati** (Lovers' grotto) to explore. *See p 46.*

⓳ **Parade in the *passeggiata.*** The early evening stroll, when everyone struts *very* slowly to see and be seen is a rite of passage in Italian life and Sicily is no exception. It's the time to socialize, people-watch, and even do business, joined in by everyone from babies to

grandparents; every town has its own version. When temperatures sizzle, Palermo's city-dwellers escape to their seaside playground in Mondello and do the ritual *passeggiata* ever so well. So dress up and join in with a *gelato* (ice cream) in hand and just walk, slowly, slowly . . . . *See p 72.*

⓴ **Eat on the waterfront at Ortygia.** Two utterly picturesque natural harbors, fresh springs, and the blessing of the Delphic Oracle have lured everyone here since Ancient Times. Treat yourself to an alfresco fishy feast perhaps of fresh tuna, swordfish, or the signature *scoppularicchi*—a mouth-watering, golden, crunchy mixture of fried squid and tiny cuttlefish. And watch the ducks as they quack their way around the papyrus in the **Fonte Aretusa** (Arethusa's Spring), the symbol of Ortygia. *See p 138.* ●

Strategies for Seeing Sicily

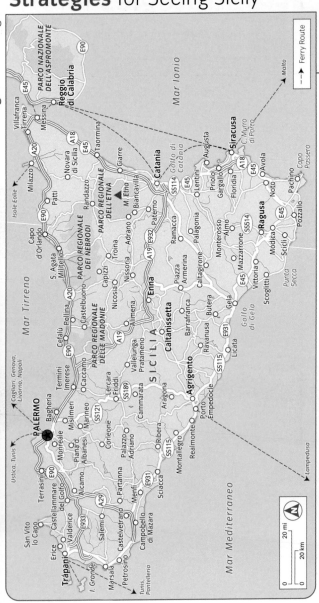

A way from the cut and thrust of the cities, rural life in Sicily tends to be enjoyed in the slow lane. There are so many sights worthy of attention that you could be forgiven for trying to visit them all. But by adopting a relatively relaxed timetable you should be able to get to the essence of the island. Here are some suggested strategies to maximize your enjoyment.

Rule #1: Have an itinerary— and an open mind

Sicily is a huge island and you may be tempted to adopt the lean-and-mean approach in an attempt to see everything. Instead, take the time to enjoy leisurely lunches and savor the scenery, and be prepared to go off the beaten track to discover your own treasured experiences. Try to limit yourself to one particular region and then explore it to your heart's content. So often, less can be more.

Rule #2: Overestimate distances

Sicily is the largest island in the Mediterranean, 177km (110 miles) north to south and 281km (175 miles) wide. Many of the loveliest parts are far from the main cities and train stations, and so it's a good idea to hire a car or, if you're feeling adventurous, a motorbike or scooter. Away from the autostrada, (highway), roads tend to be single-lane and, in more remote areas, can turn into little more than mule tracks where you may well find goats and sheep sharing the route with you. On these provincial roads sign-posting is often lacking, and so factor in extra time for finding your route; make sure that you carry a detailed road map— those supplied by car rental firms are not adequate. The best large-scale map devoted to Sicily is published by the Touring Club Italiano, available at good bookshops and, usually, at the airport. See p 163 for essential driving tips.

Explore the great outdoors.

Sicilian seafood.

Rule #3: Time it right

The best months to travel in Sicily are from April to June and mid-September to October: the weather is usually fine and not too hot, and the crowds are less bothersome. Spring can be a spectacular time to visit, when temperatures are mild and everywhere is carpeted with wild flowers. July and August is peak tourist season as well as being sizzlingly hot. Remember, too, that many Sicilians take their holidays in the last two weeks of August, which means many shops, restaurants and bars are closed—apart from on the beaches and islands. Out of high season, there are spectacular festivals, such as I Misteri in Trápani at Easter—see p 159 for a calendar of events.

Rule #4: To pack or not to pack

Even if you're packing in a lot of traveling, you can save time by basing yourself in one place and exploring the region from there, rather than hotel-flitting and having to constantly pack and unpack. Taormina and Catania are well-placed for trips around the northeast and from Palermo you can reach all the top sights quite easily. If you're visiting the interior though, you should expect to stay in different places.

Rule #5: Plan trips around lunch

When traveling from town to town, it's a good idea to arrive before lunch. Most restaurants serve from 12:30pm and, if you want to make your own picnic and stock up on supplies, bear in mind that most shops close from1pm till 4pm for the riposo (mid-afternoon closing).

Rule #6: Plot your entry point and transport

The quickest, most time-efficient way of seeing much of the island is to fly into Catania, hire a car at the airport, and travel west, ending your trip in Palermo and flying back from there. Conversely, you could fly into Palermo and end your itinerary in Catania. There is also now an international airport in Trápani on the western side of the island that has regular scheduled flights to Europe, including London. There are no direct flights from Canada and the US to Sicily, but there are regular connections from the mainland in Rome or Milan: usual flight time is 1½ hours. ●

Sicily in **Four Days**

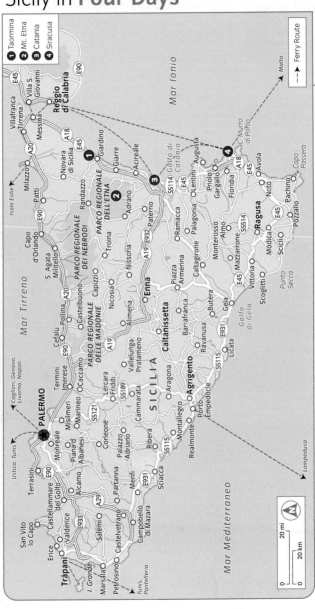

1 Taormina
2 Mt. Etna
3 Catania
4 Siracusa

--- Ferry Route

From sparkling seas and vibrant classical cities to the menacing might of Europe's most active volcano, this tour offers a taste of Sicily in microcosm: visit Taormina, the most spectacularly sited coastal town; walk on the lunar landscape of fuming, frothing Mt. Etna; see the lava city of Catania, an unsung jewel of the Baroque; and be beguiled by the beauty of Siracusa's Ortygia.

START: **Taormina. Trip length: 156 km (97 miles) ends at Siracusa.**

Travel Tip

For hotels, restaurants, and detailed information on sights in these towns, see Chapter 3 'Best Special-Interest Tours' and Chapter 6 'Best Towns and Cities'.

① Taormina. Set against the dramatic backdrop of Mt. Etna, this was once a medieval hill village, but is now famous for attracting writers, celebrities, artists, and lovers of the good life. The **Teatro Greco** (Greek Theater), carved into the hillside in 300 BC and used for Roman gladiator fights, nowadays stages summer concerts, but at all times the views of Etna, the coast, and mainland Calabria are spectacle enough. The main thoroughfare, the **Corso Umberto I**, is lined with 14th- and 15th-century *palazzi* (palaces), including Palazzo Corvaja (now the tourist office), and studded with designer boutiques, cafés, and bars. The evening *passeggiata* here—where everyone struts to see and be seen—is Sicily at its stylish best. Halfway along the Corso, the café-lined square, **Piazza IX Aprile**, is a tempting (albeit pricey) spot for a cool drink. Nearby, off the Via Bagnoli Croce, is the **Giardino Pubblico** (Public Garden) a shady oasis perched on a terrace overlooking the sea. For sun, sand, and sea sybarites, the nearest beaches are a long way below the town (accessed by cable car, bus, or steep footpath) or in the nearby resort of **Giardini-Naxos**. Taormina's excellent restaurants

generally demand deep pockets because this is Sicily's most expensive town. After your feast, bed down and head out in the morning to Mt. Etna. 🕐 *1 day. Taormina tourist office, Palazzo Corvaja, Piazza Vittorio Emanuele. ☎ 0942-23243. www.gate2taormina.com. For more on Taormina, see Chapter 6, p 143.*

From Taormina, join the A18/E45 toll road following direction Catania. After 24km (15 miles), take exit Giarre and follow the signs to Santa Venerina/Zafferana Etnea. Follow the SP92 to Rifugio Sapienza, Mt. Etna, following the brown signs (Etna & funivia). Distance: 55km (34 miles).

② Mt. Etna. Lack of volcanic eruptions permitting, it takes a good four hours to walk to the top of Mt. Etna with proper equipment such as

Corso Umberto, Taormina.

Funivia dell'Etna.

strong walking shoes or boots, fleece or padded jacket, hat, and plenty of water. Jackets and boots at €2 each can be hired at the cable car station by the **Rifugio Sapienza**

Teatro Massimo Bellini, Catania.

at the end of the road on the south side of Etna, 1,400m (4,593 ft) below the summit. For a less energetic ascent, take the **Funivia dell'Etna** cable car from the Rifugio, followed by a 4x4 mini-bus trip then a guided walk, usually to the Torre del Filó-sofo, but always dependent upon the volcano's level of activity. As well as lodgings, the Rifugio has a bar and restaurant—good for a light lunch.

After lunch, leave for Catania by mid-afternoon to get away from the city's busy outskirts before rush hour. ⏲ ½ *day. For more on Mt. Etna, see Chapter 3, p 30.*

From Rifugio Sapienza head southeast on the SP92, direction Nicolosi, follow Via del Bosco SP10 and signs to Catania. Distance: 21km (13 miles).

❸ **Catania.** After checking into your hotel in Catania, explore the center of this surprisingly compact city. The wide main boulevard, Via Etnea leads to the pedestrianized Baroque **Piazza del Duomo** and its eponymous Cathedral. Here is the city's symbol—a lava elephant topped by an Egyptian obelisk—said to protect the city from Etna's worst furies. Bars, restaurants, and enticing shops spill out from the piazza. Next morning, return to visit the **Duomo** (Cathedral), dedicated to St. Agatha, Catania's patron saint. Then head down the steps by the back of the piazza to the **Pescheria** (Fish Market) to feast your eyes on everything from huge swordfish and sea urchins to silvery anchovies. **Teatro Massimo Bellini**, to the north in Piazza Bellini, is dedicated to Catania's most famous composer, Vincenzo Bellini. Even if you don't catch a performance, guided tours are available of the opulent Sicilian Baroque interior with its near-perfect acoustics (☎ 345-2134031. Wed, Fri, Sat 10am and 11:30am; Wed, Fri 6:30pm and 7:30pm). After lunch, set off for Siracusa. ⏱ *1 day. Catania Tourist office, Via Vittorio Emanuele, 172. ☎ 800-841242. www.comune.catania.it. For detailed information, see Chapter 6, p 107.*

From Catania bear south on the SS114 then E45 toll road to Siracusa. Distance: 66km (41 miles).

4 Siracusa. Give the modern town a wide berth and concentrate on the huge Parco Archeológico della Neapolis (Archeological Park of the classical city Neapolis) for which there is a joint ticket with the Museo Archeológico (Archeological Museum). The 5th-century BC Teatro Greco (Greek Theater) is one of the world's best-preserved and largest Greek theaters—still in use for the summer festival of Greek drama and concerts. From here, it's a pleasant 10-minute stroll along oleander and citrus-tree paths to the huge ear-shaped cavern, the Orecchio di Dionisio (Ear of Dionysius), which famously amplifies sound.

Joined to the city by causeways, the tiny island of **Ortygia**—the

Enter Orecchio di Dionisio, the huge, ear-shaped cavern in Siracusa.

original heart of Siracusa with its medieval alleyways, Baroque treasures, and beautiful piazzas—is the perfect spot for strolling and dining. The **Piazza del Duomo** is one of Italy's most beautiful Baroque architectural ensembles, built on the site of a temple to Athena (c. 530 BC). Along the seafront, the **Fonte Aretusa** (Aretusa's Spring) has plenty of associated romantic legends and is one of Sicily's most photographed spots. ⏱ *1½ days. Siracusa tourist office, Via San Sebastiano, 43. ☎ 0931-481232. www.apt-siracusa. it. For detailed information on Siracusa, see Chapter 6, p 137.*

Tip

Driving on the island of Ortygia is best avoided because the narrow streets often taper to virtual dead-ends and parking areas are extremely limited. Unless your hotel has private parking, leave your car at the big garage Talete at the end of Via Trieste.

Sicily in **One Week**

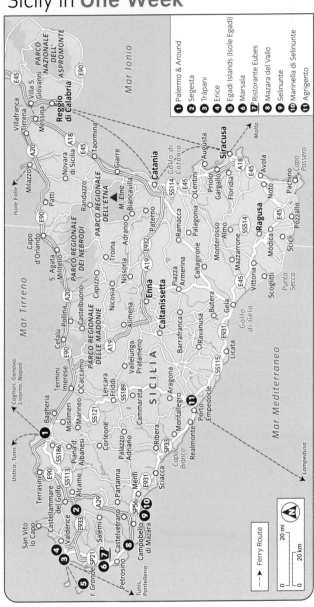

1 Palermo & Around
2 Segesta
3 Trapani
4 Erice
5 Egadi Islands (Isole Egadi)
6 Marsala
7 Ristorante Eubes
8 Selinunte
9 Mazara del Vallo
10 Marinella di Selinunte
11 Agrigento

Ferry Route

20 mi

20 km

Start in colorful Palermo, and then make trips to the island's highlights in the west and south. Monreale's Cathedral is a must-see with its glittering Byzantine mosaics. Misty, medieval Erice and Segesta's glowing Doric temple are mesmerizing. Taste Marsala's honey-colored wine, and then let the Ancients inspire and delight you in Selinunte and Agrigento's Valley of the Temples.
START: **Palermo. Trip length: 287 km (178 miles) to Agrigento.**

❶ **Palermo & Around.** Noisy, edgy, and full of colorful characters it may be, but this is a tantalizing vibrant city resplendent with handsome architecture—from ornate Baroque to Arabic, from medieval labyrinthine alleyways to Renaissance churches and palazzi. The crowning glory, at the highest point of the old city, is **Palazzo dei Normanii** (Norman Palace). Head for the Cappella Palatina (Palace Chapel) and be dazzled by the Byzantine mosaics that shine like jewels. For lunch, try the local specialties—*pasta con le sarde* (macaroni with sardines, pine kernels, and herbs) followed by Palermitan *frutta di Martorana* ('fruit' and 'vegetables' crafted from brilliantly-colored sweet almond paste). Then, before sunset take the 14½km (9-mile) drive north to **Monte Pellegrino** to savor the views of the old city and its

Spooky displays at the Catacombe of the Capuchins, Palermo.

sweeping bay. Overnight in Palermo (see Where to Stay, p 129). The next morning visit the hilltop town of Monreale 8km (5 miles) southwest of Palermo and its magnificent Duomo (Cathedral). The glittering Byzantine mosaics and medieval cloisters are truly spectacular. Head back to Palermo in time for lunch. Try to make time for the **Museo Archeológico Regionale**—one of Italy's greatest archeological museums—and the eerie **Catacombe dei Cappuccini** (Catacombs of the Capuchins) full of mummified corpses. Cool off by the **Pretoria Fountain** (also known as the 'Fountain of Shame') in **Piazza Pretoria**, before dinner. Overnight at Palermo, or take an optional trip to Cefalù 81km (50 miles) east of Palermo—one of Sicily's prettiest seaside towns. 🕐 *2 days. Palermo*

Cool off by the Pretoria Fountain.

The ancient theater in Segesta.

tourist office, Piazza Castelnuovo, 34. ☎ 091-6058351. *www.palermo tourism.com For detailed information on Palermo and Cefalù, see Chapter 6, p 123 and 112.*

To drive to Monreale take the SS186, and then the SP69 southwest of Palermo 9km (5½ miles). Leave Palermo early for the drive to Segesta on the SS113, A29: 79km (50 miles) southwest of Palermo.

❷ Segesta. The remains of the ancient city of Segesta are at their most magical early or late in the day when the light is at its best (and it's less busy). The **Doric Temple** and **Theater** are set high on a hill among flower-strewn fields and are among the most spectacularly located classical monuments in the world. From July to September summer concerts and plays are staged in odd-numbered years. Drinks, snacks, and maps of the site are available at the bar in the shop/

ticket office at the entrance. ⏱ ½ day. *Via Segesta.* ☎ *0924-955841. Segesta site open 9am to 1 hr before sunset.*

From Segesta to Trápani follow the SP33, and then the A29 dir: 41km (25½ miles) northwest.

❸ Trápani. This busy port is the departure point for ferries across to Tunisia and the Egadi Islands (see p 46)—but the old center is definitely worth a stroll. The pedestrianized main street here is called **Corso Vittorio Emanuele**, which ends at the Torre di Ligny, a squat Spanish tower. There are plenty of superb dining experiences to be had, which make Trápani a good option for an overnight stay. The highlight of the modern city is the cable car (funivia) to Erice (see ❹ below) from the Trápani terminal on Via Caserta. ⏱ ½ *day. Further information is available on* ☎ *0923-538789. www.Trápani welcom.it; see Chapter 6, p 150.*

4 Erice. The **funivia** in Trápani whisks you in 12 minutes to the enchanting, medieval hilltop town of **Erice**. From the top at 743m (2,438 ft), there are vistas along the western coast and central plains of the island right across to Tunisia's Cape Bon on a clear day. Wander around the tangle of cobbled, medieval streets then follow the path meandering along the cliff edge up to **Castello di Venere**—at the top of the town, containing vestiges of what was once a temple to Venus. Should you want to spend the night in Erice, the sunset views are spectacular and the atmosphere is especially magical once the day-trippers have left. ⏲ *½ day. Erice tourist office, Via Tommaso Guarrasi.* ☎ *0923-869388. www.prolocovald erice.it. For detailed information, see Chapter 6, p 150.*

From Trápani, take the SP21 south to Marsala. Distance: 30km (18½ miles).

Windmills and saltpans, Trapani.

Tip

High winds and swirling mists occasionally prevent the funivia from making the ascent to Erice. By road it's a 15km (9½-mile) climb with many hairpin bends—best not attempted in misty conditions. There is a regular city bus from Trápani (no. 21 or 23). But if time allows, try to wait for a clear day before visiting Erice and remember that it's always several degrees colder up there.

5 Egadi Islands (Isole Egadi). If you have time, take a ferry (1 hour) or hydrofoil (25 minutes) from Trápani to butterfly-shaped Favignana, the closest of the Egadi islands. This most accessible of Sicily's offshore isles is a great spot for swimming or simply basking in the laidback, island atmosphere. ⏲ *½ day or a full day if time permits and you want to explore Favignana town. For detailed information, see p 46.*

6 Marsala. Lying on the western-most point of Sicily, Marsala is reminiscent of a North African town, full of narrow streets and alleys. Famous for its wine, there are plenty of opportunities for tasting and supping this honeyed delight. It is famous, too, as the site where Garibaldi landed with his celebrated *Mille* ('Thousand' volunteers, see Chapter 6, p 154) in 1860 and started his campaign to make it the first city of a united Italy. Just north of Marsala is the site of the ancient Phoenician settlement, Mózia, (8th century BC)—a tiny island that is well worth a half-day visit and easily accessible by a short ferry ride from the mainland just north of town (see Chapter 3, p 52). Stay in Marsala overnight or head down to the coastal resort of Mazara del Vallo (see **8** below). ⏱ ½ *day or full day if visiting Mózia, which is a perfect spot for a picnic or lunch at the Ristorante Eubes (see 'Take a Break',* **7** *below). Marsala tourist information, Via XI Maggio, 100.* ☎ *0923-714097. www.lagunablu.org.*

From Marsala drive south on the SS115 then SP56 to Selinunte: 46km (28.5 miles). Alternatively stop at Mazara del Vallo (see **8** below). Head south on the SP21, and then SS115: 23km (14 miles).

Take a Break

7 ★★ **Ristorante Eubes.** After visiting Mózia, feast on pasta matalottea (Sicilian spiral-shaped pasta) swordfish, tuna, and all other types of fishy and traditional Sicilian delights at the Ristorante Eubes close to the little boat embarkation pier. Allow the chef Gianfranco Conticello to surprise and delight you with his dishes (no menu available—but

good appetite required): around €35 a head for a feast of many courses. *Ristorante Eubes, C. da Spagnola, 228.* ☎ *0923-996231. www.eubes.it.*

8 Mazara del Vallo. This fishing port is the most important of Sicily's Moorish towns, because it was the first to be taken by the Arabs. The Casbah (Tunisian quarter) is exotic and exciting, while the central area around Piazza della Repubblica is ringed by Baroque buildings. There is a shady *lungomare* (seaside promenade) fringed by gardens and panoramic restaurants. But the top sight is the 4th-century BC **Satiro Danzante** (the Dancing Satyr)—a bacchanalian beauty of a statue (see Chapter 5, p 79). ⏱ ½ *day. Tourist information, Piazza San Veneranda, 2.* ☎ *0923-941727. www.apt. Trápani.it.*

9 Selinunte. Perched on hills overlooking the sparkling sea, romantic Selinunte was originally one of the most powerful colonies of Ancient Greece, dating back to the 7th century BC. Traces remain of the original walled city, which was once adorned with temples. Designated by letters, the most impressive is Temple C, (6th century BC), probably dedicated to Apollo. The huge site covers 270 hectares (667 acres). With little shade, try to avoid visiting during the sizzling midday heat. ⏱ ½ *day. Selinunte Archaeological Site.* ☎ *0924-46277. www. selinunte.net.*

From Selinunte head southeast on the SS115 to Agrigento for 101km (63 miles).

To stay overnight, stop at Marinella, less than 2km (1¼ miles) down the hill to the east of Selinunte (see **10** below).

Temple C, Selinunte's most impressive monument.

🔟 **Marinella di Selinunte.** The nearest hotels to the archeological site of Selinunte are at Marinella—an attractive seaside village with a sandy beach. There's a good selection of restaurants, many of which specialize in the freshest of fish. You can see the bounty of your plate being pulled ashore off the boats at the fishing harbor. 🕐 ½ *day.*

⓫ **Agrigento.** This city is famed as the site of the ancient Greek city of **Akragus** and the celebrated **Valle dei Templi** (Valley of the Temples)—one of the most memorable sights of the Ancient World. With the exception of Greece itself, this extraordinary series of Doric temples, dating from the 5th century BC, is unrivaled throughout the world. In the eastern zone stand the eight columns of the **Temple of Heracles**, the oldest temple in the 'Valle', dating back to 500 BC. The star attraction, however, is the nearby **Tempio della Concordia** (Temple of Concord), which ranks with the Temple of Hephaestos in Athens as the world's best-preserved Greek temple. There is also an excellent **Museo Regionale Archeológico** (Archeological Museum) containing finds from the ancient city and temples. Allow a full day to do justice to the whole area. There are refreshments available at the main entrance, at the museum, and at a kiosk on the Via Sacra, or you might prefer to bring a picnic. 🕐 *1 day. Agrigento tourist information office, Piazzale Aldo Moro.* ☎ *0922-20454. www.comune. agrigento.it. For detailed information on Agrigento, see p 53.*

Sicily in **Two Weeks**

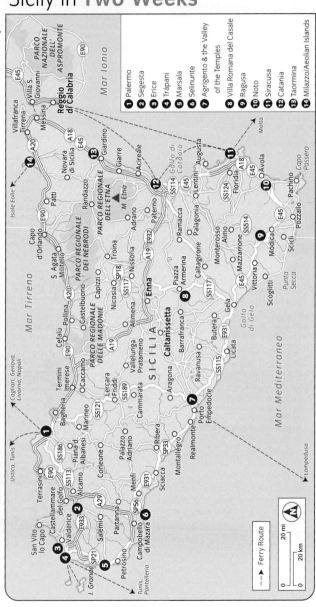

1 Palermo
2 Segesta
3 Erice
4 Trápani
5 Marsala
6 Selinunte
7 Agrigento & the Valley of the Temples
8 Villa Romana del Casale
9 Ragusa
10 Noto
11 Siracusa
12 Catania
13 Taormina
14 Milazzo/Aeolian Islands

--- ▶ Ferry Route

20 mi

20 km

This tour combines the previous trips, with some additions. Visit buzzing Palermo, and then the majestic Greek temples. From Trápani, day-trip to the Egadi Islands and medieval Erice. Inland, the Villa Romana del Casale's vivid mosaics are Sicily's greatest Roman treasures, and you can then marvel at the Baroque grandeur of Ragusa and Noto. From Milazzo sail away to the dreamy, Aeolian Islands. START: **Palermo. Trip length: 844km (527½ miles.**

Travel Tip

For hotels, restaurants, and detailed information on sights in these towns, see Chapter 6.

① Palermo. Vibrant, chaotic and utterly fascinating, Sicily's capital city plunges you into sensory overload. For a 2-day itinerary, see ① of 'Sicily in One Week'. ⏲ *2 days. For detailed information, see Chapter 6, p 123.*

From Palermo take the A29 autostrada (toll road) going southwest towards Trápani and exit at Segesta. Distance: 75km (47 miles).

② Segesta. The majestic **Tempio of Segesta** is one of the world's most perfectly preserved temples, built in the 5th century BC but mysteriously left unfinished. For a half-day itinerary, see ② of 'Sicily in One Week'. ⏲ *½ day. For detailed information, see Chapter 3, p 51.*

From Segesta return to the A29 and continue west to Erice. Distance: 44 km (27 miles).

③ Erice. Explore the cobbled streets of Sicily's most fairytale medieval town, perched on a hilltop with sweeping vistas from Mt. Etna to Tunisia. Be sure to taste the specialty *dolci ericini* (sweet marzipan and almond candies and cakes), or shop for the locally made *frazzate* (bright cotton rugs), which make superb souvenirs. For a half-day itinerary, see ③ of 'Sicily in One

Week'. ⏲ *½ day. For detailed information, see Chapter 6, p 150.*

From Erice, head southwest on two unmarked but signposted roads to Trápani. Distance: 14km (8¾ miles).

④ Trápani. Spend the morning in this busy portside town whose fortunes were traditionally made from tuna fish, salt, and carved coral. Today only the salt industry continues to thrive alongside the port with its regular ferries and hydrofoils to the nearby Egadi Islands and Tunisia. For a half-day itinerary, see ④ of 'Sicily in One Week'. ⏲ *½ day.*

Enjoy the architecture and vibrate culture of Palermo.

Sweet marzipan treats in Erice.

From Trápani, drive south along the SP21 to Marsala. Distance: 31km (19 miles).

5 **Marsala.** Stay overnight here, to take in a tour of one of the wineries for which the town is so famous, and enjoy a few tastings of Marsala wine. Try Florio, the oldest and most famous winery at Via Vincenzo Florio, 1; ☎ **0923-781111**; www.cantineflorio.com. For a half-day itinerary, see **6** of 'Sicily in One Week'. ⏰ *½ day. For detailed information, see Chapter 6, p 154.*

From Marsala, drive south on the SS115 and then SP56 to Selinunte. Distance: 46km (28¾ miles).

6 **Selinunte.** Let your imagination be your guide as you approach Selinunte for the first time, recalling that it was once a splendid Greek colony whose walled city encased many glorious temples. For a half-day itinerary, see **9** in 'Sicily One in Week'. ⏰ *½ day. For detailed information, see Chapter 2, p 53.*

From Selinunte, head southeast on the SS115 to Agrigento. Distance: 101 km (63 miles).

7 **Agrigento & the Valley of the Temples.** Arrive at sunset to see these remarkable ancient temples at their best, or after dark when the site is floodlit. Perhaps stay overnight nearby, and return early in the morning to explore the ruins further. For a 1-day itinerary, see **11**

Florio, the oldest winery in Marsala.

in 'Sicily in One Week'. ⏱ *1 day. For detailed information, see Chapter 2, p 53.*

From Agrigento, drive east on the SS115, winding along the coast to the city of Gela. From here head northeast on the SS117 bis to Piazza Armerina. Distance: 124 km (77½ miles).

❽ Villa Romana del Casale. Just 6km (3 ¾ miles) southwest of Piazza Armerina is one of Sicily's greatest and best attractions—the 3rd-century AD **Villa Romana del Casale** (☎ 0935-686667; www. villaromanadelcasale.it). Buried and protected by muddy deposits until 1950, excavations revealed the finest Roman mosaic floors that are unique for both their extent and quality. It's thought that the villa was originally used as a hunting lodge, hence the vividly-colored mosaics of animals and birds. It is also, famously, the site of the mosaic depiction of the world's first bikinis, with 10 scantily dressed girls performing gymnastic activities. Have a snack outside the Villa's main entrance, before the drive to Ragusa for the night. ⏱ *½ day. For detailed information, see Chapter 3, p 54.*

From Piazza Armerina, head southeast towards Ragusa on the SS117, followed by the SS124 and SS154. Distance: 91km (56¾ miles)

❾ Ragusa. This superb Baroque city is in two parts—the **Upper Town** and **Ragusa Ibla**. After the ravages of the great earthquake of 1693, Ragusa Ibla has risen phoenix-like from the ashes as one of Sicily's most perfectly restored Baroque towns. Its winding streets are studded with beautiful old *palazzo* and lodgings ranging from chic B&Bs to deluxe hotels. ⏱ *½ day (full day if possible). Ragusa Ibla Tourist*

Temple of Conchord, Agrigento.

Information, Via Capitano Bocchieri, 33. ☎ 0932-221511. www.ragusa turismo.it. For detailed information, see Chapter 6, p 132.

From Ragusa, drive east to Noto on the SP55, and then pick up the SP18 and SS115. Distance: 55km (34 miles).

❿ Noto. With its honey-colored stone, Noto vies with Ragusa Ibla as Sicily's most perfect Baroque town (both are **World Heritage Sites**). Have lunch here before setting off for Siracusa. ⏱ *½ day. Noto Tourist Information, Piazzale XVI Maggio. ☎ 0931-896654. www.comune. noto.sr.it. For detailed information, see Chapter 6, p 118.*

From Noto to Siracusa, head southeast and pick up the A18 going north and then the SS124. Distance: 38km (24 miles).

⓫ Siracusa. Be sure to see Siracusa, once the most powerful city in the world and, according to the

Siracusa's waterfront and harbor.

Roman orator Cicero (106–43 BC), 'the most beautiful of all the Greek cities'. For an itinerary, see ❹ of 'Sicily in Four Days'. ⏱ *2 days. For detailed information, see Chapter 6, p 137.*

From Siracusa to Catania, go north to pick up the E45 and then SS114 all the way. Distance: 87 km (54 miles).

⓬ **Catania.** Sicily's second city is another must-see. With fewer historical sights than Palermo, it boasts some fine Baroque architecture and a more cosmopolitan atmosphere. It is also a good lunch stop, with plenty of fine restaurants and cafés. After eating, head for the southern slopes of Mt. Etna. For an itinerary, see ❷ and ❸ of 'Sicily in Four Days'. ⏱ *1 day. For detailed information, see Chapter 6, p 107.*

From Catania to Taormina, take the autostrada A18 all the way. Distance: 53km (34 miles).

⓭ **Taormina.** Sicily's best-known resort has beguiled visitors for at least three millennia and remains the island's most chic destination. Its best beach is the **Lido Mazzarò** (see Chapter 4, p 69). For an itinerary, see ❶ of 'Sicily in Four Days'. ⏱ *1 day. For detailed information, see Chapter 6, p 143.*

From Taormina to Milazzo, pick up the A18/E45 autostrada and then the A20 exit Milazzo/Isole Eolie. Distance: 85km (53 miles).

⓮ **Milazzo/Aeolian Islands.** Don't linger long in the port of Milazzo—it's simply a convenient departure point for the idyllic, volcanic Aeolian Islands (Isole Eolie). If you're short of time, take a daytrip to Vulcano, the closest of the seven isles, to watch the smoking main crater and wallow in therapeutic mud baths. Lípari, the main island, boasts a lively resort—Lípari Town. But most spectacular of all is Strómboli whose crater seethes and fumes constantly with, usually, nightly displays of pyrotechnics from one of the world's most active volcanoes. ⏱ *3 days. For detailed information see Chapter 3, p 43.* ●

The Best Special-Interest Tours

Sicily for **Foodies**

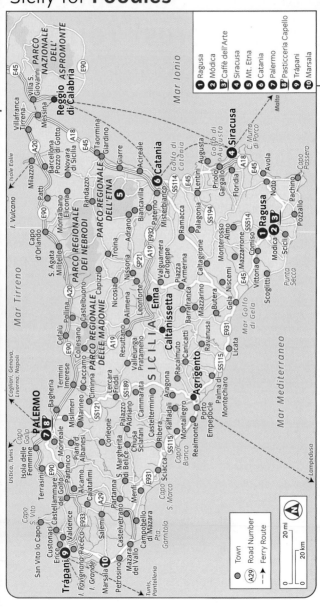

1 Ragusa
2 Módica
3F Caffè dell'Arte
4 Siracusa
5 Mt. Etna
6 Catania
7 Palermo
8F Pasticceria Capello
9 Trápani
10 Marsala

Town
(A29) Road Number
--→ Ferry Route

0 ___ 20 mi
0 ___ 20 km

This sun-drenched, fertile land has a rich gastronomic tradition. The Greeks introduced olives, and also grapes for their wines. The Arabs imported sweet and spicy tastes, the Spanish added tomatoes and chocolate, and the French brought a legacy of chefs for the aristocracy. Today a feast of flavors awaits you in Sicily and it's rare to eat anything that isn't produced locally. START: Ragusa. Trip length: 7 days.

Travel Tip

For recommended hotels, see Chapter 6.

❶ ★★★ **Ragusa.** The province of Ragusa is 'the garden of Sicily' where most of the island's vegetables and fruit are grown. Greenhouses allow year-round production and the land is speckled with almond and olive groves. Be sure to taste *mandorle* (almonds) in a cooling *granità* (crushed ice), for which the Sicilians are so famous. The honey-color stone of Ragusa Ibla's Baroque buildings is replicated in the local golden honey that is used to sweeten desserts. Then there's the great variety of cheeses: try the tangy pecorino, fragrant *provola*, and robust *caciocavallo*, sprinkled over pasta dishes.

For carnivores, Ragusa is famed for its unusual and creative meat dishes, especially beef, pork, mutton, and rabbit. *Coniglio all'agrodolce* is sweet and sour rabbit, marinated in olive oil, rosemary, bay leaves, and red wine. An ideal accompaniment is the local red Cerasuolo—among Sicily's top wines with a distinctive, delicate hint of cherry. ⏱ *3 hrs. Ragusa Ibla tourist office, Via Capitano Bocchieri, 33.* ☎ *0932-221511. www.ragusaturismo.it.*

From Ragusa, drive south on the N194 following the signs to Módica. Distance: 18km (11¼ miles).

Specialities of Ragusa.

❷ ★★★ **kids Módica.** Módica is famed not only for its Baroque architecture, but also for its chocolate, known as *cioccolato di vetro*— glass chocolate. Made traditionally using Aztech methods introduced by the Spanish, sugar and pure cocoa are combined in low temperatures into a grainy, crunchy texture with flavorings such as vanilla and cinnamon—or peppercorns and chilies for spicier tastes. If you're feeling especially adventurous, the local specialty *mpanatigghi* are unique little pastries filled with veal

Olive trees grow in the fertile soil around Mount Etna.

and Módica chocolate. Sample them all at the **Antica Dolceria Bonajuto** (Corso Umberto I, 159; ☎ 0932-941225; www.bonajuto. it). Founded in 1880, this is Sicily's oldest chocolate manufacturer where you can indulge in free chocolate tastings and visits by appointment. 🕐 *2 hrs.*

3 ★★ kids **Caffè dell'Arte.** This café makes an ideal stop for light refreshments. It has been delighting taste buds with its pastries and 'glass chocolate' since 1967. And, if the Lacono family owners are making chocolate on the day of your visit, you may well be invited to take a peek at the process. *Corso Umberto I, 114.* ☎ *0932-943257. $.*

From Modica drive south on the N115 to Ispica and continue on N115 north following the signs to Siracusa. Distance: 73km (46 miles).

4 ★★★ kids **Siracusa.** Overlooking the Ionian Sea, it's no surprise that fish is the great culinary inspiration here. Fresh tuna, swordfish,

and *scoppularicchi*—a golden mixture of fried squid and tiny cuttlefish—are sublime, while signature sauces for pasta include *vermicelli alla siracusana* combining glossy eggplants (aubergines), yellow peppers, zucchini (courgettes), and tomatoes with black olives, capers, and anchovies.

You'll be spoilt for choice with cafés and seafood restaurants on the picturesque waterfront in **Ortygia** (see p 138), but for a real gastronomic experience head just inland to the excellent restaurant **Don Camillo** (see Chapter 6, p 141), set in the vaults of a former 15th century monastery. 🕐 *full day. Siracusa tourist office, Via Maestranza, 33, Ortygia.* ☎ *0931-464256. www.apt-siracusa.it. (and see Chapter 6, p 137 for more information on Siracusa).*

From Siracusa drive north on the E45, and then join the N114 and follow the brown signs for Etna Sud and Rifugio Sapienza. Distance: 100km (62 miles).

5 ★★★ kids **Mt. Etna.** The exceptionally fertile soil of this much loved and feared volcano produces a number of gastronomic treasures: there is succulent kid (young goat) from Randazzo, olives from Biancavilla, cherries from Macchia, and sausages and pulses from Linguaglossa. And the volcano's flanks are cloaked with thick chestnut woods where wild mushrooms flourish. West of Etna, Bronte is surrounded by groves of pistachio trees. Nearby, Maletto is famous for strawberries—renowned as Sicily's sweetest. There is a strawberry festival on the first Sunday in June when the streets are alive with processions through the streets. ⏱ *4–5 hrs. Etna Sud Tourist Office, Rifugio Sapienza.* ☎ *095-916356. www. parcoetna.ct.it.*

From Mt. Etna, exit south and join the A18 signposted Catania. Distance: 43km (27 miles).

⑥ **Catania.** For an unforgettable introduction to the sights, sounds, and gourmet delights here, join the throng at the fish market **La Pescheria** (just beneath Piazza del Duomo open Mon–Sat 5–11am). Stalls groan under mountains of the bounty of the sea, from gleaming swordfish to twitching octopus and

squid, freshly shucked oysters, mussels, sea urchins, and countless other fishy delights. Off the main street, Via Etna, the **Fera o Luni** (Piazza Carlo Alberto, open Mon–Sat from 7am), is a colorful, boisterous market with tasty morsels galore, such as *alivi cunzati* (olives with chilli, pepper, and pickles) or *calia e simenza* (roasted chick peas and pumpkin seeds)—perfect for eating on the hoof.

Catanian specialties include *risotto nero*, rice cooked in dark cuttlefish ink (sometimes with tomato sauce on top to emulate a volcanic eruption from Etna) and *pasta alla Norma*, named after Vincenzo Bellini's operatic heroine—a pasta sauce made of eggplants (aubergines), tomatoes, and fresh ricotta. It was in Catania province, too, that the tradition of Sicilian ice creams and sorbets was born, using mountain snow from Etna, mixed with juice or flower essence and sugar. *Catania tourist office, Via Cimarosa, 10.* ☎ *095-7306233. www.apt.catania.it.*

From Catania take the A19/E932 and follow the signs for Palermo. Distance: 210km (131 miles).

Catania Fish Market.

Volcanic Wines From Etna

Growing grapes on the flanks of an active volcano can be a risky affair. But a great bonus of the mineral-rich volcanic soil combined with sand is that phylloxera, the mite that destroyed most of Europe's vineyards in the 19th century, could not exist under mighty Etna. As a result, some very old vines remain on their original roots—a rare thing in Italy. These wines have freshness, richness, and complex aromas, and include rosés, dry whites, and red wines. The whites use the Malvasia, Catarratto, and Minella grape varieties, some of which are up to 100 years old. The rosso (red) wines have a minimum of 80% of Nerello Mascalesse—an ancient vine cultivated in Etna for 400 years—which is a deep black grape with spicy notes and produces a soft, full-bodied wine. For a tour of one of Etna's vineyards, telephone Frank Cornellisen on ☎ 392-9769728.

7 ★★★ **kids Palermo.** Elaborate cuisine meets simple, home-grown fare in the capital city. Everywhere

Market stall selling spices and nuts in Palermo.

you go the Arab influence recalls the exotic influences and traditions. The specialty is *pasta con le sarde*—sardines, pine nuts, saffron, raisins, wild fennel, toasted breadcrumbs, and anchovies simmered and served with pasta, usually the long, hollow *bucatini* pasta (deriving from *buco*, meaning hole).

The Palermitani also love fried foods. Buy a cone of *gameberetti fritti* (fried shrimps) or *calamaretti* (tiny squid)—dusted in flour and fried with a squeeze of lemon, to eat as finger food. And visit at least one of the three most important markets. The **Mercato della Vucciria** (east off Via Roma, Piazza Caracciolo) is the oldest and most famous where huge swords arch skywards of the *pesce spada* (swordfish) and, in summer, immense *tonno* (tuna) are carved into thick steaks by the dexterous and vociferous stall-holders. The scene is no less theatrical at the **Mercato del Capo** and at the **Mercato di Ballarò** (Via Ballarò & Piazza del Cármine). Palermo has some of Sicily's best *pasticcerie* (cake shops) where you can indulge including lobster, gray mullet, grouper, swordfish, squid, cuttlefish, and tuna. For centuries tuna fishing has been an integral part of the area's history with the bloody *mattanza* (tuna massacre, see p 47) providing the main ingredient for countless recipes. *For more information* ☎ *0923-538789. www.trapani welcome.com.*

From Trápani, follow the SP21 signposted Marsala. Distance: 30km (18¾ miles).

🔟 ★★ **Marsala.** Marsala is the home of the world-famous Marsala wine, a rival of port and Madeira. It can be sweet, dry, or spicy—much more versatile than a sweet dessert wine. *Marsala Tourist Information, Via XI Maggio 100, (off Piazza Repubblica).* ☎ *0923-714097 (see Chapter 6, p 154, for more information.*

Palermo has some of the best cake shops in Sicily.

in a *cannolo* (fried pastry oozing with ricotta, sugar, and chocolate) or *cassata* (sponge cake). 🕐 *half or full day. Palermo Tourist Office, Piazza Ca\stelnuovo, 34.* ☎ *091-6058351. www.palermotourism.com. For more information, see Chapter 6, p 123.*

Florio's attractively packaged Marsala wine.

8 ★★ **Pasticceria Capello** has some of Palermo's best cakes and pastries. Try the divine sette veli (seven veils)—a sublime version of chocolate heaven, with seven layers from dark to white, crunchy to soft, chocolate. *Via Colonna Rotta, 68 (near Palazzo dei Normanni).* ☎ *091-489601. www.pasticceria cappello.it.*

From Palermo, take the E90/A29 then the SP21 following signs to Trápani. Distance: 111km (69 miles).

9 ★ **Trápani.** Here the Arab influence is at its strongest and couscous (known locally as *cuscus*) is the prince of local specialties and symbol of the province. Try it steamed in fish broth, *cuscus con pesce*. Fish takes pride of place on local menus,

Best **Natural Phenomena**

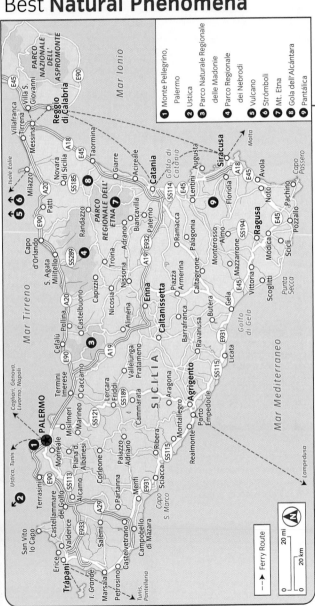

1. Monte Pellegrino, Palermo
2. Ustica
3. Parco Naturale Regionale delle Madonie
4. Parco Regionale dei Nebrodi
5. Vulcano
6. Strómboli
7. Mt. Etna
8. Gola dell'Alcántara
9. Pantálica

Thisis landscape that ignores anything in between lascivious softness and damned harshness,' wrote Giuseppe di Lampedusa about his island in Sicily's most famous novel, *The Leopard* (1958). Europe's highest, most active volcano, 1,000 kilometers of coastline sprinkled with islands, lofty mountains, and luxuriant woods, lakes and gorges, all serve to stimulate every sense in this dramatic land. START: **Monte Pellegrino (15km (9 miles) north of Palermo). Trip length: 10 days.**

❶ ★★ **Monte Pellegrino, Palermo.** This limestone mountain, 600m (1,968ft) high, forms a dramatic backdrop to Palermo. Locals revere it as the holy mountain because it's the site of a shrine to St. Rosalia, the patron saint, who lived and died here as a hermit in the 12th century. But inhabitants date back to 7000 BC and cave drawings from the Palaeolithic and Neolithic periods have been discovered in the **Grotta dell'Addaura** (northern side of Mt. Pellegrino; ☎ **091-6961319,** closed at time of writing

owing to rock falls). Casts of the engravings can be seen in Palermo's **Museo Archeologico Regionale** (see Chapter 6, p 155). ⏲ *1 hr.*

Drive down into Palermo to the Stazione Maríttima for the year-round ferry service (not on Sundays in winter) to Ustica operated by Siremar (Via Francesco Crispi, 118. ☎ 091-582403. www.siremar.it). Journey time 2hr 40 minutes by ferry or 1hr 15 minutes by hydrofoil (hydrofoil operates from April–December).

Monte Pellegrino, Palermo.

2 ★★ kids **Ustica.** Roughly 56km (35 miles) north of Palermo lies the turtle-shaped tip of a submerged volcano—the oldest little island (8.7 sq km/3.36 sq miles) in the Sicilian outer archipelago. Its black lava landscape is daubed with vividly colored flowers and the rugged coastline indented with coves and grottoes. Take a boat trip round the island and don't miss the **Grotta Azzurra**—named after the famous cave in Capri and sharing the same iridescent glow of blue light reflected from the sea. Designated Italy's first marine reserve in 1986, it's also an underwater paradise of coral and colorful fish from little anemones to big groupers—claimed by some divers to be as big as a Fiat 500 car—and turtles, which are now a protected species. ⏱ *1 day. For details of activities including boat trips contact Centro Accoglienza per la Riserva Marina (Marine Reserve Visitors' Centre), Piazza Umberto, 1.* ☎ *091-8449456.*

Parco Regionale dei Nebrodi.

Back in Palermo, join the autostrada A19 going east following signs to Cefalù. Take the Buonfornello exit and head east on the coastal SS113 to Campofelice di Roccella, and then turn off for Collesano inland for the Parco Naturale Regionale delle Madonie. Distance: 89km (55½ miles).

3 ★★ **Parco Naturale Regionale delle Madonie.** Often called a 'botanic paradise', this park holds more than half of the island's 2,600 plant species. Ancient rocks are interspersed with spectacular mountains, including **Pizzo Carbonara** (1,979m /6,493ft), the highest mountain in Sicily after Mt. Etna. There are farms and flower-filled meadows where the tinkling of cowbells is never far away and several charming villages such as the mountain-ringed **Petralia Sottana**—the park's HQ, which provides superb information about walks. ⏱ *½ day. Parco delle Madonie. Corso Paolo*

Agliata, 16, Petralia Sottana.
☎ *0921-684011. www.parcodelle
madonie.it.*

Follow the road back to the coast
and pick up the A20/E90 signposted Messina going east. Follow the SS113 with signs to
Acquedolci and then the SS289 to
Parco Regionale dei Nebrodi. Distance: 132km (82½ miles).

❹ ★★ Parco Regionale dei
Nebrodi. Sicily's largest park covers an area of 85,687 hectares
(330.8 sq miles) extending east to
west for 70km (43½ miles). From the
high peaks you may be able to spot
golden eagles wheeling on the ther-
mals and several species of griffon
vultures spying hungrily down upon
you. This wilderness was once the
habitat of hippopotamus, elephant,
and rhino—all long gone—but now
you can walk in the tracks of porcu-
pines, wildcats, and indigenous San
Fratello horses. This is also Europe's
largest remaining beech forest.
Shimmering lakes, often with views
of fuming and frothing Mt. Etna,
make it one of the most naturally
scenic areas of the island. There are
few roads and villages and a car is
essential for exploring the wild land-
scapes and long distances. The park
office at Cesarò (Strada Nazionale;
☎ 095-696008; www.parks.it/parco.
nebrodi) has maps and detailed
information. Just north of here on
the winding SS289 road is Monte
Soro (1,847m/6,058ft), the highest
point of the Nebrodi. ⏲ ½ day.

Tip

The town of Cesarò bursts into a
flurry of horses' hooves and equine
dexterity on 15th August every year
in the Palio dei Nebrodi horse race
(see p 160).

Head northeast on the SS289 and
rejoin the coastal road A20 east,
following signs to Milazzo/Isole
Eolie, the embarkation point for
the Aeolian Islands. Distance:
128km (80 miles).

❺ Vulcano. The closest island of
the Aeolians to the Sicilian 'mainland'
was, according to legend, the home
of Vulcan, the god of fire and the
gateway to Hades. There's no mistak-
ing the inspiration for these hellish
legends: the searingly bright yellow,
orange, and red sulfur-stained rocks,
acrid fumaroles, sulfur-belching Gran
Cratere (Big Crater), and muddy
baths brimming with naked bodies.
There are three dormant volcanoes
on the island—Vulcanello, Saraceno,
and Aria—but the fourth, Gran Cratere, still smokes and steams even
though the last eruption was in 1890.
It's quite a stiff scramble to the rim of
the huge crater 391m (1,283ft) high,
from where you can look down into
the infernal abyss. Tickets for the
ascent cost €3. Allow a couple of
hours for the round trip. Near to the
docks the Laghetti di Fanghi or
mud baths (Easter–Oct daily 7am–
9pm; €2) are a pit of greenish-yellow
sulfurous mud, reputed to relieve
rheumatism and certain skin dis-
eases. It also stings terribly if you get
it in your eyes. The mud is unsuitable
for young children or pregnant
women and you may also like to take
a peg for your nose as the smell is of
the most rotten of eggs. ⏲ ½ day.

❻ ★★★ Strómboli. Permanently
active, Strómboli is the youngest
volcano on the Aeolian Islands—we
get the term 'strombolian' from
here, meaning short, explosive outbursts of lava and ash ejected high
into the air. The explosions come
from the mouths of the three main
craters at an altitude of 701m
(2,300ft) in the high part of the
Sciara del Fuoco (Slope of Fire), on

Take a dip in the mud baths of Volcano.

the western side of the island. At night you can often see the glowing red-hot lava snaking its way down

Fishing boats on Strómboli Island.

the slope and hear the loud hiss as it meets the sea.

Until the great eruption of 1930, there were about 5,000 permanent island dwellers, now there around 400. There were major eruptions in 2002 and 2003 causing tsunami waves and damage to houses, and in 2007 an eruption resulted in the formation of two new craters on the summit. By law, the cone of the volcano, **Gran Cratere**, can be visited only with a guide and visits are restricted to 80 people on the summit at any one time, so it's wise to book an organized excursion as soon as you can. **Magmatrek** (just off the piazza at Via Vittorio Emanuele; ☎ **090-9865768**; www.magmatrek.it) has treks throughout the year led by Mario Zaìa and his volcano guides, charging €25 per person. They lead groups on the three-hour one-way trip up the mountain, usually leaving at 5pm or 5:30pm in summer (at 4pm in spring and fall) and returning at 11pm.

(You do need to have a good level of fitness because it's quite a scramble and I don't recommend taking the trip during the day—it's far less dramatic then). For a more leisurely spectacle, take a boat trip at night to see the Sciara del Fuoco (book at the harbor stands for boats leaving at 10pm for the 2½ hour trip, at around €20 per person).

From Milazzo, drive east on the E90, and then the A20 & A18 following signs for Catania then Zafferana/Etnea/Pedara on the SP92. Distance: 140km (87½ miles).

❼ ★★★ kids Mt. Etna. Europe's largest and most active volcano holds the world record for eruptions and has been called the greatest pyrotechnic show on earth. And yet, this fire-breathing dragon which is capable of destroying everything in its wake, is loved and deeply respected by the locals as a good and kind mountain.

Ask any mountain guide why *il vulcano*—masculine in Italian—is called 'she' and the reply comes 'Etna is like a woman—dangerous and mysterious—just like a beautiful woman.' La *Signora Etna* is worshipped; people make offerings and bless their houses to escape her wrath. Even when she is venting full fury, wiping out all obstacles in her path, hapless homeowners, forced to abandon their dwellings, leave bread, cheese, and wine to satisfy and appease her. After all, even gods of destruction need rest and food.

The first rumblings began around 1500 BC. The Sicels, original inhabitants of Sicily, worshipped Adranus the fire god who was said to live under the volcano before being driven out by the Greek god Vulcan who made it into his forge. His groanings and hammerings accounted for the violent, earth-shaking eruptions. Today it is Europe's highest volcano—and a highlight of any trip to Sicily—towering at 3,300m (10,827ft) with a perimeter of 160km (100 miles).

Dramatic clouds gather over Mt. Etna.

During the major eruptions in 2001 and 2002–3, seas of lava cascaded downhill sweeping through the middle of the mountain hut, Riugio Sapienza, wiping out the cable car that ran to the top, engulfing three of its pylons and melting its cables. Etna pumped so much ash and red-hot molten rock into the sky that it forced the closure of Catania airport, 25km (16 miles) away.

Bocca Nuova ('the new mouth') is the youngest of Etna's craters, all of which are active. In November 2006, it eclipsed the others in a spectacular show of power and heat. Showers of glowing lava were accompanied by fiery explosions—*lapilli* of molten rocks. Strombolian fountains erupted every second reaching 200m (656ft) high. Snow melted in a trice with air temperatures soaring from minus 5°C (23°F) to more than 40°C (104°F) and ribbons of steam hissed through the funneling wind. ⏱ *½ day. For more information, see Chapter 2, p 30.*

Take a cool walk at the Gola dell'Alcántara.

From Mt. Etna National Park, drive northwards and the Gola dell'Alcántara is on the SS185 between Francavilla and Castiglione di Sicilia. Distance: 58km (36¼ miles).

8 ★★ kids **Gola dell'Alcántara.** This spectacular gorge is the perfect place to cool off in the icy, clear waters of the Alcántara River. In fact, this is not one but several gorges, created by a lava flow from Mt. Etna thousands of years ago. Now designated as a protected area, the **Parco Fluviale dell'Alcántara** (☎ **0942-985010**; www.parco alcantara.it; open daily; €5 for lift down into the park; waders available for hire) has extraordinary rock formations. There's also a free public entrance 200m (656ft) past the lift entrance—but be prepared for the 200 steps down—and, crucially, back up again. ⏱ *3–4 hrs.*

Tombs in the limestone rocks at Pantàlica.

Tip

The gorge tends to get very busy in summer and at weekends, so for a less crowded visit drive on to Francavilla di Sicilia following the brown signs to Le Gurne and park in the old center by the church of Santa Maria Assunta.

Tip

There are marked paths and mule tracks following the Alcántara river: 'A' is for easier paths, 'B' for more challenging ones. There are plenty of idyllic picnic spots where you can feast among citrus trees, prickly pears, and wild flowers, and enjoy the scenery of plunging ravine and sheer rock faces.

From the Gola dell'Alcántara, head south on the A18/E45 signposted to Catania, and then continue on the E45 after the Catania turn-off. Take the SS114 following the signs for Ragusa, and then the S194 to Ferla. Drive uphill through Ferla following the brown tourist signs to Pantálica and park at the Castello del Principe entrance. Distance: 136km (85 miles).

⑨ ★★ Pantálica. This Bronze Age necropolis is Sicily's largest and most important. More than 5,000 tombs are honeycombed into the limestone rock at the **Necrópoli di Pantálica** (open 9am–sunset; free). Now a UNESCO World Heritage Site, it is estimated to date from the 13th–8th centuries BC and believed to have been the pre-Greek settlement Hybla of the Siculi people, whose skeletons were contained within the caves. There are easy, although sometimes rocky, paths around the area meandering through holm oak and willow and, in spring and summer, the grass is sprinkled with wild orchids. ⏱ *1 hr.*

Best **Islands**

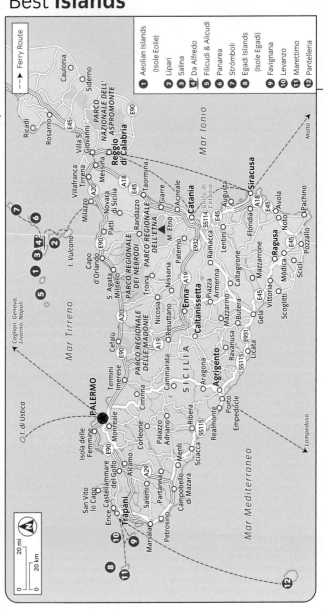

--- ▶ Ferry Route

1. Aeolian Islands (Isole Eolie)
2. Lipari
3. Salina
4. Da Alfredo
5. Filicudi & Alicudi
6. Panarea
7. Stromboli
8. Egadi Islands (Isole Egadi)
9. Favignana
10. Levanzo
11. Marettimo
12. Pantelleria

As well as being the largest island in the Mediterranean, Sicily owns several island archipelagos. The magnificent seven volcanic Aeolians Islands all have UNESCO World Heritage status. To the west, turtle-shaped Ustica has Sicily's best-preserved marine reserve and the Egadi Isles bask in shimmering seas. Closer to Tunisia than Sicily, chic Pantelleria is the largest island. START: **Aeolian Islands**. Trip length: 10 days.

Tip

The only Aeolian islands where you might need a car are Lípari and Salina—otherwise best to leave it in a garage on the mainland, and there are several at Milazzo, including Central (☎ 090-9282472) or enquire at the tourist office in Milazzo, just behind the harbor at Piazza Duilio, 20 (☎ 090-9222865).

❶ ★★★ kids **Aeolian Islands (Isole Eolie).** The Ancient Greeks believed that these seven islands were the home of Aeolus, god of the winds. Legend says that he lived in a cave on **Vulcano**, the island that gave its name to all volcanoes. This is usually your first port of call on the ferry or hydrofoil and it is worth spending several hours here. The highlight is the walk up to the impressive, smoking crater, **Fossa di**

Vulcano, and a wallow in the evil-smelling **Fanghi**—mud baths—see 'Natural Phenomena', p 35. ⏱ ½ day. *Vulcano tourist office, Via Provinciale 41. ☎ 090-9852028. Open Jun–Oct 8am–9pm.*

❷ **Lípari.** Like all the Aeolian Islands, Lípari is the offspring of volcanic eruption, but although now dormant, it makes up for this with great scenic beauty—sitting on a plateau of red, volcanic rock. This, the biggest island, has more tourist facilities than any of the other Aeolians, and makes a good base for exploring the archipelago. Lípari is also the name of the island's only real town, enclosed by walls built by the Spanish in the 16th century. The main sights are the **Duomo** (cathedral) and the star attraction the **Museo Archeologico Eoliano** (☎ 090-9880174; daily 9am–1:30pm & 3–7pm: entrance €6). This museum counts

Lípari Harbor.

among one of Europe's most important prehistoric and classic collections, showcasing the early settlers and traders who inhabited these islands for 7,000 years. Elsewhere there are beautiful walks and, unusually for these volcanic islands, a beach **Spiaggia Bianca** (White Beach) north of Lipari Town, so called because of the pumice dust from the quarries that lends the sea a dazzling shade of aquamarine). When night falls, head for the waterside **Marina Corta** to one of the open-air bars—perfect for people-watching and gazing across to nearby Vulcano. ⏲ *1 day. Lipari tourist office, Corso Vittorio Emanuele, 202.* ☎ *090-9880095. www.aasteolie.info.*

❸ **Salina.** Salina achieved worldwide fame as the setting of the 1995 film *Il Postino*, where the postman of the title learns to love poetry after befriending the exiled Chilean poet Pablo Neruda: 'Poetry doesn't belong to those who write it—it belongs to those who need it'. This idyllic island *is* the stuff of poetry, shaped by two (extinct) volcanoes, where exuberant vegetation alternates with dark volcanic cliffs that plunge to the sea past little white houses and vineyards. It is a fertile and tranquil island, seemingly

unaffected by its status as a magnet for A-list celebrities and their yachts (such as Jennifer Lopez, Sting, and Tom Cruise). It is undoubtedly a place to walk slowly, savor the views, good beaches and high class lodgings, and enjoy Slow Food. The Slow Food Movement was born in Italy in 1986 and is dedicated to countering fast-food culture. Its manifesto urges us to 'rediscover the flavors and savors of regional cooking and banish the degrading effects of fast food'. ⏲ *½ day.*

❹ ★★ **Da Alfredo.** This little café on Salina reputedly serves the best fresh fruit granita in the world. Treat yourself to a mouthwatering crushed ice and lemon juice. Apparently, it's as good for you as it is delicious because supposedly something in Sicilian lemons allows red blood cells to absorb more oxygen. *Piazza Marina Garibaldi, Lingua (on the southeastern side of the island).* ☎ *090-9843075. $.*

Tip

Set in the center of the archipelago, Salina is a good jumping off base for

The unspoilt island of Alicudi.

Panarea church and gardens.

exploring the other islands and is about 25 minutes by hydrofoil from Lipari.

5 **Filicudi & Alicudi.** These two little westerly islands are delightfully unspoiled and the wildest of the Aeolians. **Filicudi** is the larger of the two, but still has only about 300 permanent residents. Although this island has no sandy beaches, there are plenty of rocky coastal stretches and a pebbly beach with superb swimming in crystalline waters. **Alicudi** is the most remote and least populated of all the islands. There are no roads and electricity and TV arrived only in the 1990s, but there is a sprinkling of houses, a couple of shops, and one hotel and restaurant. For lovers of complete quiet and relaxation, this is paradise. ⏱ *1 day.*

6 **Panarea.** Northeast of Lipari, **Panarea** is the smallest and most chic of the Aeolians and the setting for many of Italy's richest families' holiday homes. Some say it's also the prettiest, known locally as the 'isle of flowers'. Three villages cluster together on the eastern side of the island—Ditella, Drauto, and San Pietro—the latter being where all

the boats dock. There's a popular, sandy beach below Drauto, and nearby at the headland of Punta Milazzese is a Bronze Age village of 23 huts, discovered in 1948. At *aperitivo* time, the terrace of the Hotel Raya is *the* place to be (Via San Pietro; ☎ 090-983013; www.hotelraya.it)—a magnet for the international jetset in understated luxurious style. The hotel's disco keeps the island awake till dawn—but only in August. Out of season, the island is a quiet haven with beautiful walks and only a few small electric cars to disturb the peace. ⏱ *1 day.*

7 **Stromboli.** Probably the most famous and spectacular of the Aeolian Islands, it is certainly one of the most active volcanoes in Europe and well worth an ascent to the top for the nightly fireworks show (see p 37). If you want to follow in the incendiary tracks of Ingrid Bergman and her lover, director Roberto Rossellini, who came here in 1949 to make the film *Stromboli,* and get up close and personal to the volcano, you'll need to spend the night on the island. Stromboli town is the main settlement and a pleasant place for a stroll around the **Piazza San Vincenzo** from where there

The tiny island of Strombolicchio.

Cala Rossa, Favignana.

are splendid views of **Strombolic-chio**—a tiny basalt island topped with a lighthouse. Have a drink and snack at **Ritrovo Ingrid** (Piazza San Vicenzo; ☎ **090-986385**), named in honor of 'La Bergman' and festooned with old movie posters. Nearby, just past the church of **San Vicenzo**, is the *casa rossa* (red house) where Ingrid lived with Roberto Rossellini in 1949. The only thing recording the liaison—scandalous at the time because Rossellini was married—is a plaque recording the bare facts. ⏱ *2 days.*

From Milazzo, drive west and take the A20 and then E90, and follow the signs to Trapani onto the A29. Distance: 308km (192 miles). From the Stazione Marittima in Trápani, car ferries operated by Siremar depart for the Egadi Islands all year round, taking approximately 45 minutes to Favignana (Siremar ☎ 0923-545455; www.siremar.it). Hydrofoils (*Aliscafi*) are also operated by Siremar and Ustica Lines (☎ 0923-22200; www.usticalines.it). They leave from Via Ammiraglio Staiti (east of the Stazione Marritima) and take 20 minutes to Favignana and Levanzo, approximately 1 hour to Marettimo.

Hydrofoils run at regular intervals from 7:30am (weather permitting) and one-way fares are from €6.60 (Favignana & Levanzo) and €11.80 (Marettimo) plus booking fee. The ticket office is at Via Staiti, 23 (the main road opposite the port entrance).

⑧ ★★ Egadi Islands. These are the most accessible of Sicily's offshore islands and, in spite of their long history, the three beauties have remained largely unchanged over the years. There are still isolated coves and bays, deserted mountain paths to hike, and a slow pace of life. It's possible to visit any of the three on a day trip from Trápani, but it is also worth considering a longer linger, for which you should book your lodgings well in advance for summer vacations. ⏱ *1 day.*

⑨ Favignana. The largest of the Egadis is called *La Farfalla* after its 'butterfly' shape. As the closest island to the mainland—just 16km (10 miles) away—it can become very crowded in high season. It's highest point is **Monte Santa Caterina** (287m/942ft) to the west, but the east side of the island is flat and hiring a bicycle is a great way to explore (see Chapter 5, p 76). Look for *Noleggio bici* signs everywhere advertising bike rental shops. The only town is also called Favignana and has two piazzas and plenty of shops specializing in the local specialty—tuna. Even today these islands are home to the largest tuna fishery in Sicily and the ancient ritual of **La Mattanza**, the bloody slaughter of the local tuna, takes place in May and June. This is a spectacle not for the faint-hearted, but some fishermen offer boat tours for glimpses of the bloody action. Contact the tourist information center (below) for details.

The greatest magnet to this island is the excellent swimming in the crystalline waters in bays such as **Cala Rossa** at the island's eastern end. And there are also spectacular caves, such as the **Grotta Azzurra**, **Grotta dei Sospiri** (meaning 'sighs'), and even the **Grotta degli Innamorati** (Lovers' grotto), all accessible by boat tours. ⏰ ½ day. *Favignana tourist office, Piazza Madrice, 78.* ☎ 0923-921647.

🔟 **Levanzo.** The smallest of the Egadis is just north of Favignana and perfect for walking, swimming, boating, and enjoying life in the slow lane. The coastline is indented with caves, including the **Grotta dei Genovesi** with its extraordinary

prehistoric rock art. You need to arrange your visit through the custodian, Signor Castiglione at Via Calvario, 11 (near the hydrofoil quay (☎ 0923-924032/339-7418800). If the sea is calm and the wind low you can visit by boat, usually departing at 10:30am and 3:30pm and lasting two hours. Alternatively, an excursion in off-road 4x4 vehicles also takes around two hours and involves a fairly tough descent on foot to the grotto. Expect to pay €15 either by boat or 4x4 for the standard excursion.

Levanzo Town is the main settlement, with just two hotels and restaurants and a couple of little shops. ⏰ *1 day.*

⓫ **Marettimo.** Known to the Greeks as 'the sacred island', Marettimo is also the most isolated, mountainous, and greenest of the Egadis. Limestone cliffs plummet toward the cobalt-blue sea within which lie the remains of the Carthaginian fleet destroyed by the Romans in 241 BC. The coastline is peppered with caves, including the **Grotta del Presepio** where wind and sea-sculpted stalactites and stalagmites look as though they've stepped out of a Christmas crib. There's a handful of restaurants, all

Pre-historic rock art, Grotta dei Genovesi.

The coastline of Marettimo is peppered with caves.

naturally specializing in the 'catch of the day'. Try **Il Veliero** by the harbor for a truly fishy feast. ⏱ *1 day. Via Umberto, 22.* ☎ *0923-923274.*

Getting to Pantelleria: From Trapani there are daily overnight car ferries all year round (departure Trapani 11:59pm, arrival in Pantelleria 6:45am) operated by Siremar (☎ 0923-545455; www.siremar.it). Ustica Lines (☎ 0923-22200; www.usticalines.it) have hydrofoil crossings from Trapani (passengers only) daily from 10th June–10th October, departing 6pm and arriving 8:30pm. You can also travel by hydrofoil with Ustica Lines from Mazzara del Vallo daily from 1st July–31st August, departing 8:15am, arriving Pantelleria 10am. Distance: 48km (30 miles). Hydrofoils for both routes cost around €36 one-way with booking fee extra. Ferries are around €32 one-way.

By air you can fly from Trapani with Meridiana (☎ 0789-52682; www.meridiana.it, three flights per day). Air One also flies from Palermo (☎ 02583-25035; www.flyairone.it). Check websites for best prices.

⑫ ★★ **Pantelleria.** Sicily's largest island is known as the 'Black Pearl of the Mediterranean'—nothing to do with Jack Sparrow's fictional ship in *Pirates of the Caribbean*, though. The Arabs called Pantelleria *Bint-al-Rion* (Daughter of the Wind) and, true to its old name, breezes often buffet the rocky shores. They also conveniently keep the temperature below sizzling point in summer and nudge away rain clouds in winter. But they don't deter a galaxy of famous visitors, from Aldous Huxley and Truman Capote (who found literary inspiration) to current celebrities and fashionistas who come here to be immersed in its beauty. ⏱ *2 days.*

Sicilian Menu Terms

Abbacchio Roast haunch or shoulder of lamb baked and served in a casserole and sometimes flavored with anchovies.

Anguilla alla veneziana Eel cooked in a sauce made from tuna and lemon.

Arrosto Roasted meat.

Baccalà Dried and salted codfish.

Bocconcini Veal layered with ham and cheese, then fried.

Bollito misto Assorted boiled meats served on a single platter.

Braciola Pork chop.

Cacciucco ali livornese Seafood stew.

Cappelletti Small ravioli ("little hats") stuffed with meat or cheese.

Carciofi Artichokes.

Cozze Mussels.

Fagioli White beans.

Fave Fava beans.

Fontina Rich cow's-milk cheese.

Fritto misto A deep-fried medley of whatever small fish, shellfish, and squid are available in the marketplace that day.

Mortadella Mild pork sausage,(can also be made of donkey), fashioned into large cylinders and served sliced.

Mozzarella con pomodori (also caprese) Fresh tomatoes with fresh mozzarella, basil, pepper, and olive oil.

Osso buco Beef or veal knuckle slowly braised until the cartilage is tender and served with a highly flavored sauce.

Panettone Sweet yellow-colored bread baked in the form of a brioche.

Panna Heavy cream.

Pappardelle alle lepre Pasta with rabbit sauce.

Piselli al prosciutto Peas with strips of ham.

Pizzaiola A process in which something (usually a beefsteak) is covered in a tomato and oregano sauce.

Polenta e coniglio Rabbit stew served with polenta.

Polla alla cacciatore Chicken with tomatoes and mushrooms cooked in wine.

Pollo alla Marsala Chicken cooked in Marsala wine.

Pollo all diavola Highly spiced grilled chicken.

Scaloppine Thin slices of veal coated in flour and sautéed in butter.

Semifreddo A frozen dessert; usually ice cream with sponge cake.

Sogliola Sole.

Spiedini Pieces of meat grilled on a skewer over an open flame.

Stufato Beef braised in white wine with vegetables.

Tonno Tuna.

Tortelli Pasta dumplings stuffed with ricotta and greens.

Trenette Thin noodles served with pesto sauce and potatoes.

Vitello tonnato Cold sliced veal covered with tuna-fish sauce.

Zuppa inglese Sponge cake soaked in custard

The **Ancient World**

1. Solunto
2. La Muciara
3. Segesta
4. Mózia
5. Selinunte
6. Agrigento
7. Villa Romana del Casale
8. Morgantina
9. Tíndari

--→ Ferry Route

Sicily is a great, unique repository of classical treasures, such as the vast collection of Greek ruins, perfectly preserved temples, Roman monuments rivaled only by those of Rome itself, together with prehistoric, Phoenician, and Carthaginian remains. More Greek temples survive here than in Greece itself and ancient Mózia is the world's best-preserved Phoenician site. **START: Solunto is 20km (12½ miles) east of Palermo. Trip length: 7–10 days.**

1 Solunto. Perched on the edge of Monte Catalfano, overlooking the fishing town Porticello, this location is spectacularly wild. Solunto was built by the Phoenicians in about 700 BC as one of their earliest trading posts on the island. The Carthaginians followed, eventually to be usurped by the Romans in 254 BC, only to be abandoned during the 3rd century AD, probably as it failed to become wealthy. The site was only re-discovered in 1825 and

excavations have continued ever since. Traces of all three civilizations remain and, although no complete buildings remain, you can get a good sense of the layout from the Roman *decumanus* (main street) and the remains of the villas and their original mosaic floors. A highlight in the Casa di Leda is a mosaic of Zeus in the guise of a swan seducing Leda. ⏱ *1 hr.* ☎ *091-904557. Admission €3. Mon–Sat 9am–6pm, Sun 9am–1pm.*

2 ★★ La Muciara. Enjoy a fresh fish and seafood lunch down in the nearby fishing village Porticello—especially popular with the locals on Sunday. *Via Roma,103.* ☎ *091-957868. $$.*

From Porticello, take the A19 and then the E90 to Palermo. Follow the A29 signposted to Trápani, A29 dir and take the exit for Segesta. Distance: 101km (62¾ miles).

3 Segesta. Standing alone, high on a hill, surrounded by unspoiled rolling green countryside with views to sigh for stretching to the sea, the **Doric Temple** here is arguably the world's most stunningly-sited classical monument. In the 12th century, Egesta (now known as Segesta) was the main city of the Elyminans, legendary survivors of the Trojan war who also founded Erice (see p 150). But the remarkably well-preserved **Doric Temple** was the work of the later Greek colonists around 430–420 BC when Segesta had a profitable commercial alliance with Athens. It has 36 Doric columns

9.33m (31ft) high, but remained unfinished without the typical Doric fluting on the columns and without a roof. No ancient writings survive to tell the true story as to why it was abandoned. Try to visit in the early morning or late afternoon when the stone glows gold and the scent of wild flowers, fennel, and rosemary is intoxicating.

The Theater lies across from the Temple on the top of Monte Barbaro. Dating probably from the mid-3rd century BC, it accommodated 3,200 spectators The glorious views from here are the perfect backdrop to the plays and other events that are still staged here during the summer months. ⏱ *3 hrs. Area Archeologica Di Segesta, Via Segesta.* ☎ *0924-952356. Admission €6). Daily Nov–Mar 9am–4pm, Apr–Aug 9am–7pm.*

Tip

Although access to the Temple is relatively easy up a series of shallow steps, it is quite a steep walk uphill to the Theater from the ticket office (1½km/1 mile), but a shuttle bus runs every 30 minutes from the ticket office—cost €1.50.

Doric Temple, Segesta.

Temple E, Selinunte.

From Segesta, go west on the SP33, and then the A29 dir & SP21 signposted to Trapani/Marsala. Take the SS187 following brown signs marked 'Isole Stagnone' and turn left following sign 'imbarco per Mózia' (embarkation point for Mózia) to the ferry landing stage. Distance: 50km (31 miles).

❹ **Mózia.** A little ferry boat chugs across to the **Stagnone Nature Reserve**—home to an idyllic mini archipelago, the centerpiece of which is the tiny island of San Pantaleo. Here, you will find the site of **Mózia (Motya),** the island of the Phoenicians. In the 8th century BC, Motya (Mózia in Italian) was the most important Phoenician trading post in Italy. By 398 BC it was abandoned when the Phoenicians moved to Lillybaeum (Marsala) as their new headquarters. Centuries later, the Englishman Pip Whitaker (1850–1936), a Marsala wine merchant and amateur archeologist, bought the island and began the first excavations, which yielded Mózia's extraordinary history. Follow the aloe-lined footpaths around the little island (2½km/1½ miles in circumference)

to see the **Casa dei Mosaci** with its splendid black and white mosaics depicting animal scenes such as a winged gryphon attacking a horse (3rd century BC). Look out also for the submerged **Phoenician causeway** that connected the north gate of the town to the mainland, allowing carts and horses to seemingly glide across the water. On the left is the necropolis and **Tophet** (a sacrificial place), dedicated to the goddess Tanit, where the Phoenicians are believed to have sacrificed their first-born children and animals. Highlights of the **Whitaker Museum** include a large collection of pottery, jewelry, glassware, and *stelae* (grave markers), all excavated locally, together with **Il Giovinetto di Mózia**—a remarkable early 5th-century BC life-size marble sculpture of an athletic youth, who may have been a charioteer or even a god—only discovered in 1979 by Nino Montelione, who's often to be found at the ticket office. 🕐 *3 hrs. Museo Whitaker.* ☎ *0923-712598. €9 for ferry access to island and museum. Daily 9:30am–1:30pm and 2:30–6:30pm; reduced hours during winter.*

Tip

Mózia is a great spot for a picnic, set among the rich macchia (maquis) on the island and where vines are also grown. Next to the Whitaker Museum, there's an enoteca (winebar), where you can taste the island wines.

From Mózia, take the SS115 south to Marsala, and then to Mazara del Vallo. Follow the SP56 to Selinunte. Distance: 60km (37½ miles).

⑤ Selinunte. Wild celery (*selinon* in Greek) lent its name to this colony, set on a high plain among wildflowers and fragrant herbs in a spectacular location overlooking the sea. Abandoned for over 2,000 years, its numerous temples, acropolis, and agora lie in dignified ruins across a vast site. The ticket office is near the **East Temples** (E, F, and G), which stand in a group. The most stunning is **Temple E,** a Doric building dating to the 5th century BC (but reconstructed in 1958) and probably dedicated to Aphrodite. Down a long track you come to the Acropolis and **West Temples** (A, B, C, D, and O). **Temple C** is the site's earliest and best preserved monument. Although its glorious frieze panels are now in Palermo's Archeological Museum (see Chapter 6, p 126), 14 columns have been re-erected. If you want to explore the whole site (270 hectares/667 acres) you should allow up to 4 hours and be prepared to walk in the heat of the sun. However, **Ecotour4Venti** (☎ 0924-941208;

www.ecotourselinunte.com) have electric carts that take you around the site: opt either for Eastern Hill (30 minutes for €3) or the whole site (1hr for €6). (☎ *0924-46251. www.selinunte.net. Admission €6). Daily 9am–1 hr before sunset.*

From Selinunte, take the SS115 east, past Sciacca, and follow the brown signs to Agrigento. Distance: 101km (62 miles).

⑥ Agrigento. In Greek Sicily, Siracusa (see p 137) may have been the most powerful city but Agrigento was the richest and most luxurious. Modern day Agrigento is blighted by charmless tenement-style apartment blocks, but there is one sight, you should not miss: the **Valle dei Templi** (Valley of the Temples). The **archeological park** is a UNESCO World Heritage Site consisting of eight temples (and various other remains) built between about 510–430 BC. In the **Eastern Zone** the **Temple of Hercules** (6th century BC) is the oldest and you can wander freely. Just past it is the star of the site, the **Temple of Concord** (430 BC) one of the world's best-preserved Greek temples with 34 columns. It's not possible to wander freely inside here, but it is a marvel of serenity and balance. If time is limited, try also to see the **Temple of Hera**, (partly destroyed by an earthquake in the Middle Ages) and, in the **Western Zone**, the **Temple of Olympian Zeus** which, although unfinished and now badly crumbled, was the largest Doric temple ever known—about the size of a football pitch. Another must is a visit to the

Mosaic in the Agrigento Archeology Museum.

impressive finds of the **Museo Archeológico**. ⏱ ½ day. Archeological park. ☎ 0922-621611. www.parcovalledeitempli.it. Admission €8). Daily 8:30am–7pm, also open at night in July and Aug. Museo Archeológico Via dei Templi, halfway up the road from the archeological park. ☎ 0922-401565. Daily 9am–7pm. Admission €6. Cumulative ticket for archeological park & museum €10.

From Agrigento, drive east to join the SS640, and follow the SS191 through the Barrafraca signs to Piazza Armerina. Villa Romana del Casale is on the right 5km (3 miles) southwest of Piazza Armerina. Distance: 98km (61 miles).

7 Villa Romana del Casale.
This UNESCO World Heritage Site is Sicily's best, most important treasure trove of Roman remains—and among the most beautiful and extensive mosaics in the world.

The villa dates from the late 3rd or early 4th century AD, and many scholars believe that it belonged to Maximilian, Diocletian's co-emperor who ruled between AD 286–305. In the 12th century it was almost completely engulfed in a mudslide and lay largely buried till treasure was found in 1950 and excavations began in earnest. They revealed a vibrant snapshot of the loves and lives of the aristocracy during the decline of the Roman Empire. Everything from hunting and sport to feasting, dancing, and lovemaking is depicted in the mosaics. Raised walkways circle the interior from where you can view the scenes. Don't miss the massive 'Corridor of the Great Hunt' mosaic depicting the capture of wild animals destined for the gladiatorial circuses of Rome under the watchful eye of the bare-bosomed Queen of Sheba; or the Sala delle Dieci Ragazzi (Room of the Ten Maidens) where the girl gymnasts appear to be wearing bikinis (long before Coco Chanel's invention in the 1950s).

The best time to visit the villa is early or late in the day due to the crowds and the perspex covering to protect the mosaics, which creates hothouse conditions. ⏱ 2 hrs. ☎ 339-2657640/0935-680036. www.villaromanadelcasale.it. Admission €3; free to EU citizens under 18. Daily 10am–6pm.

The well-preserved theater at Morgantina.

The Santuario di Tindari.

Tip

The nearby town of Piazza Armerina holds the thrilling horse race, the Palio dei Normanni on 12th, 13th, and 14th August, a must if you're in the area. This event, a competition of knightly combat and horsemanship, records the heroics of the Norman invaders who ousted the Arabs from Sicily in around 1060.

Drive 15km (9½ miles) northeast to Morgantina.

⑧ **Morgantina.** Extensive, yet relatively off the tourist trail, this former Greek city was at the height of its powers in the 4th century BC. Morgantina is an evocative sight, framed by pine and olive smothered blue-gray hills. The hilltop **Cittadella** (citadel)—site of a Bronze Age settlement—is studded with chamber tombs and has an ancient form of shopping mall in the *macellum* (enclosed market). The old downtown center is the Agora (marketplace) and, on the right, the well-preserved **Teatro** (Theater) dates from the 3rd century BC. So far only about a fifth of the city has been excavated. ⏱ *1 hr.* ☎ *0935-87955. Admission €3. Daily 9am–1 hr before sunset.*

Drive east towards Catania and follow the A19, and then the A18 to Taormina. Distance: 116km (72 miles).

⑨ **Tindari.** Driving along the coastal road, you'll notice a temple perched on a rock high above the sea: the **Santuario di Tindari**. Erected to the Black Madonna, who was said to have performed miracles, it's now a place of pilgrimage, but also the site of the ancient Greek town, Tyndaris. The **archeological site** (☎ *0941-369023*; open 9am–1 hr before sunset; €2) was one of the last Greek settlements on the island, founded in 396 BC. Most of the remains are on the north-western side overlooking the sea where there are Roman baths and villas with floor mosaics and ingenious heating systems. Carved into the hillside the well-preserved **Teatro** (theater) was built in the late 4th century BC, and then adapted by the Romans for their gladiatorial style of theater. Here in summer (June–August) Greek plays and concerts are staged. For tickets, check with the ticket office at the entrance or call the box office. ⏱ *1 hr.* ☎ *0941-243176. www.teatroduemari.net.*

Historic **Architecture**

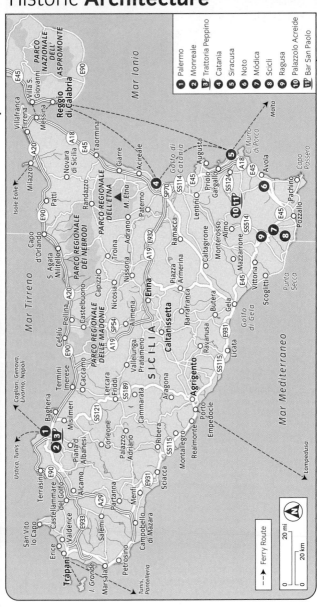

1 Palermo
2 Monreale
3▸ Trattoria Peppino
4 Catania
5 Siracusa
6 Noto
7 Módica
8 Scicli
9 Ragusa
10 Palazzolo Acreide
11▸ Bar San Paolo

Mar Ionio

Malta

Golfo di Catania

Capo Passero

Mar Tirreno

Isole Eolie

Ustica, Tunis

Cagliari, Genova, Livorno, Napoli

Mar Mediterraneo

Lampedusa

Tunis, Pantelleria

PARCO NAZIONALE DELL' ASPROMONTE

PARCO REGIONALE DEI NEBRODI

PARCO REGIONALE DELL' ETNA

PARCO REGIONALE DELLE MADONIE

SICILIA

Reggio di Calabria

Messina

Villa S. Giovanni

Villafranca Tirrena

Milazzo

Patti

Capo d'Orlando

S. Agata Militello

Cefalù

Termini Imerese

Caccamo

Bagheria

Misilmeri

Pianad'Albanesi

Corleone

Palazzo Adriano

Castellammare del Golfo

Terrasini

Alcamo

Partanna

Menfi

Sciacca

Ribera

Montallegro

Realmonte

Porto Empedocle

Agrigento

Cammarata

Aragona

Vallelunga Pratameno

Caltanissetta

Barrafranca

Butera

Gela

Licata

Ravanusa

Piazza Armerina

Enna

Nissoria

Nicosia

Troina

Adrano

Paternò

M. Etna

Randazzo

Novara di Sicilia

Taormina

Giarre

Acireale

Catania

Augusta

Priolo Gargallo

Lentini

Caltagirone

Monterosso Almo

Mazzarrone

Vittoria

Scoglitti

Punta Secca

Golfo di Gela

Pozzallo

Pachino

Avola

C. Murro di Porco

San Vito lo Capo

Erice

Valderice

Trápani

Salemi

Petrosino

Marsala

Campobello di Mazara

I. Grande

Castelbuono

Pollina

Lercara Friddi

Capizzi

Almenia

Ramacca

Grammacca

Ferry Route

20 mi

20 km

0

E45
E90
E45
A20
A18
A19
A29
E931
E932
E933
SS114
SS115
SS121
SS124
SS189
SS514
SP54
SP70

Always the prized island of the Mediterranean, for centuries Sicily has been subjected to foreign rulers. One of their tourism advertising slogans even read 'Come and invade us—everyone else has!' But this odyssey of troubled times has left a superb mix of architectural styles throughout the land to inspire and delight.

① Palermo. Artistic delights are round every corner, from the Normans' great contributions of the cathedral at Monreale and the Cappella Palatina in the Palazzo dei Normanii, to Arabic flamboyant decoration and even extravagant Baroque and Renaissance buildings. Indeed, Palermo's Arab-Norman buildings have no equal anywhere in the world (for more information, see Chapter 6, p 123).

Palermo's greatest architectural treasure is **La Cappella Palatina** in the **Palazzo dei Normanni** (Piazza Indipendenza,1; ☎ **091-7054317**; Mon–Sat 8:30–noon and 2–5pm; Sun am only; €6) whose interior is completely smothered in glittering 12th-century mosaics. **Piazza Bellini** has two jewel-box ancient churches showing the fusion of Norman and Arab design: the 12th-century **Chiesa della Martorana** contains some of the most impressive mosaics on the island and the tiny **Church of San Cataldo,** remarkable for its Moorish tomato-red domes on top of a church of Christian design. Note that both churches are closed at lunchtime (usually from 2–3:30pm, but these times can change). ⏲ *1 day.*

From Palermo, Monreale is 8km (5 miles) southwest on the SP69. But a better option is to take Bus 389 that runs frequently from Piazza dell'Indipendenza (about 20 minutes; fare €1.20).

② Monreale. Overlooking the valley of the **Conca d'Oro** ('Golden Shell'—so called because of its extensive orange orchards) is the

Mosaic of Christ in the Duomo di Monreale.

Piazza del Duomo, Catania.

highlight of any Arab-Norman odyssey. The **Duomo di Monreale** is the best example of Norman architecture in Sicily, founded by William II as a glittering palace of Byzantine mosaics, rivaled only by Istanbul's Santa Sofia. Inside, the mosaics stretch in glorious golden expanses along the walls covering almost 8,000 sq m (86,111 sq ft). A full 2,200kg (4,850 lbs) of pure gold were used, and the stories from the Old and New Testaments were created by Byzantine and Arab craftsmen. Outside the Cathedral (on the right from the front) is the entrance to the **Cloister.** This is an exquisite Islamic-style ensemble of graceful arches encircling a garden planted with olives and bay trees, and framed by 228 slender inlaid columns. Look for the fine **fountain** in the south-west corner, reminiscent of a palm tree. At the top are decorations of 12 figures, some dancing, others playing musical instruments. King William ll (1166–89) was reputed to refresh himself at this fountain every morning. ⏱ *½ day. Cathedral, Piazza Duomo.* ☎ *091-*

6404413. Admission free but take €1 coins for lighting up the mosaics. Daily 8:30am–12:30pm and 3:30–6pm. Cloister, Chiostro dei Benedettini Piazza Guglielmo il Buono. ☎ *091-6404403. Admission €6. Daily 9am–6:30pm.*

3 ★ **Trattoria Peppino.** This is a good place for an alfresco lunch off the main tourist drag, hidden away in a side street off the Via Roma. Home-made pizzas and pasta and more substantial dishes are on the menu. *Via B. Civiletti, 12.* ☎ *091-6407770. \$\$.*

From Monreale, drive east to pick up the A19 and then the E45 signposted Catania. Distance: 218km (136 miles).

4 **Catania.** Dominated by Mt. Etna, Sicily's second city has always been subjected to the might and wrath of the volcano, most devastatingly in the 17th century when boiling lava spewed forth covering everything; then in 1693 when a mighty earthquake shook it to its foundations. The old part of town was rebuilt in the Baroque style with wide, open *piazze* and avenues— and the material used was lava, making it a truly unique city. The center of town is the **Piazza del Duomo** with all its surrounding buildings designed by the Palermitan architect Giovanni Battista Vaccarini. (Best not to mention this though to the Catanians, who are arch rivals of Palermitans). ⏲ *1 day. For more information, see Chapter 6, p 107.*

From Catania, head south on the **SP70, and then the E45 and SS124 to Siracusa. Distance: 66km (41 miles).**

⑤ **Siracusa.** Founded by the Greeks in 733 BC, Siracusa rapidly rose to become the most powerful city in Europe. The **Parco Archeológico della Neapolis** is on the mainland in the northwest of town. The highlight of all the extraordinarily well-preserved Greek and Roman remains is the **Teatro Greco.** Built in the 5th century BC, it could accommodate 15,000 spectators and 59 of the original 67 rows of seats remain—used for the annual Greek theater festival and concerts (mid-May to end of June). The **Orecchio di Dionisio** (Ear of Dionysus) is an ear-shaped grotto, which according to legend was used by the tyrant of Siracusa (Dionysus) to listen to prisoners' conversations. The excellent acoustics allowed him to eavesdrop from outside. The island of **Ortygia** is packed with over 2,500 years of history and architectural styles from classical times to medieval Norman and Baroque. ⏲ *1 day. Parco Archeológico della Neapolis, Viale Teocrito, 66.* ☎ *0931-65068. Admission €6. Tues–Sun 9am–7pm. For more information on Siracusa, see Chapter 6, p 137.*

Tip

There's a colorful, bustling morning street market (Mon–Sat) on Via Trento in Ortygia (turn left at the entrance to Ortygia), and an excellent delicatessen for food and wine delights at the end of the market, Sapori dei Gusti Smarriti ('the flavors of lost tastes').

Drive south, signposted to Noto, on the A18. Distance: 38km (23¾ miles).

⑥ **Noto.** Another victim of the terrible earthquake in 1693, Noto was rebuilt about 10km (6 miles) from the old center and in 2002 was added to UNESCO's World Heritage list. Known locally as *Il Giardino di Pietra* ('Garden of Stone'), the local limestone takes on a soft peachy-golden glow and the effect, especially at sunset, is spectacular. This is a town of small scale and symmetrical proportions and the Sicilian pinnacle of Baroque architecture and town planning. The three architects responsible for this near perfect Baroque town were Paolo Labisi, Vincenzo Sinatra, and Rosario Gagliardi. Yet the stone is also fragile and a survey in 1986 revealed that even the slightest tremor could destroy the buildings. ⏲ *½ day. See Chapter 6 for more information, p 118.*

Sculpture, Ortygia.

Tip

At the end of May, Noto celebrates the arrival of summer with a very colorful festival called the Infiorita, in which flower artists create elaborate mosaics using petals.

Drive west following the SS115 signposted to Modica. Distance: 37km (23 miles).

⑦ Módica. Sitting at the bottom of a gorge among limestone hills, this town is a site of pilgrimage for lovers of the Baroque—and of chocolate (see p 29). It's divided into the higher and lower towns, **Modica Alta** and **Modica Bassa** respectively, linked by many flights of steps. Be sure to visit the flamboyantly decorated 18th-century **Church of San Giorgio** in Modica Alta (open daily but closed at lunchtime), created by the Baroque genius architect, Rosario Gagliardi, and the **Cattedrale di San Pietro** (just off Corso Umberto in Modica Bassa, open daily) at the top of

dizzying steps, lined with statues of the apostles. ⏱ *½ day. Modica tourist information, Via Grimaldi, 32.* ☎ *0932-762626. Mon–Sat 8:30am–1:30pm & 3–7pm, Sun 8:30–1:30.*

Tip

The access road (SS115) passes over the 300m (984ft) high Guerrieri bridge giving spectacular views of Modica deep below, where the Baroque buildings appear to be stacked on top of one another.

From Modica, go southwest on the SP54 in the direction of Scicli. Distance: 10½km (6½ miles).

⑧ Scicli. Off the tourist trail, but now becoming better known, this appealing Baroque town is set in attractive countryside, dominated by lofty limestone cliffs. Take time to wander around this country town, past **Palazzo Beneventano** (just off Piazza Italia)—whose monster-adorned balconies are worth a look—and the nearby, curvaceous

Church of San Giorgio, Módica.

church of San **Bartolomeo** (open daily). The **Via Mormino Penna** is also well worth a stroll, lined with *palazzi* and Baroque churches. ⏱ *2 hrs.*

From Scicli, follow the SP54 going north signposted to Ragusa. Distance: 25km (15½ miles).

❾ **Ragusa.** Like its neighbors in the Val di Noto, Ragusa was decimated by the earthquake of 1693. The town is part of the Val di Noto Heritage site and 18 of its buildings are protected by UNESCO. There are two separate parts of town— **Ragusa Superiore,** stretching out over a mountain plateau—and **Ragusa Ibla,** also Baroque but built along the labyrinthine streets of the former medieval town. If time is limited, confine yourself to Ragusa Ibla where historic golden limestone buildings are being renovated and very chic hotels and restaurants are opening. Dominating the **Piazza del Duomo** is the **Basilica di San Giorgio** (open daily), built in 1738 by Rosario Gagliardo, with its tiered wedding-cake appearance. The impressive neoclassical dome was added in 1820. ⏱ *½ day. For more information, see Chapters 5 & 6, p 98 & 132.*

From Ragusa, go south on the SP54 and then the SS115 to Palazzolo Acreide. Distance: 25km (15 ½ miles).

❿ **Palazzolo Acreide.** Also on the UNESCO World Heritage list, this slightly rough-round-the-edges Baroque town also fell victim to the great earthquake of 1693. It is nonetheless a very pleasing town, whose origins date to the 12th century BC under the Siculi, and it is currently undergoing a major make-over. The heart of town is the **Piazza del Popolo,** around which are three striking Baroque churches. Just off

Ragusa Ibla.

the piazza, the **Casa-Museo di Antonio Uccello** is the former home of the eponymous poet (1922–79), who dedicated his life to the preservation of Sicily's rural past. Above the town the ruins of the Ancient Greek **Akrei** (☎ 0931-881499; daily 9am–7pm; admission 2€; see Chapter 5, p 95) are also worth exploring. ⏱ *2 hrs. Palazzolo Acreide tourist information, Palazzo Municipiale, Piazza del Popolo. ☎ 0931-882000. www.palazzolo-acreide.it. Mon–Sat 9:30am–1pm and 3:30–6:30pm. Casa-Museo di Antonio Uccello, Via Macchiavelli, 10. ☎ 0931-881499. www.antonio uccello.it. Admission free. Daily 9am–1pm.*

⓫ **Bar San Paolo.** Treat yourself here to a taste of the local foodie specialty, impanata: crispy bread stuffed with vegetables, such as broccoli, potato, and onion, or sun-dried tomatoes. *Piazza Umberto.* ☎ *0931-882300. $.*

Best for **Children**

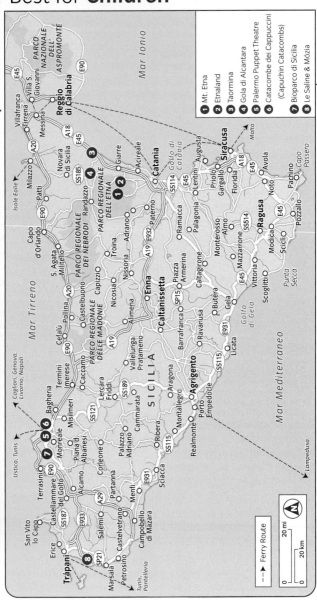

1. Mt. Etna
2. Etnaland
3. Taormina
4. Gola di Alcantara
5. Palermo Puppet Theatre
6. Catacombe dei Cappuccini (Capuchin Catacombs)
7. Bioparco di Sicilia
8. Le Saline & Mòzia

Volcanoes, theme parks, hide and seek behind Doric columns, splashing around in water, crabbing in rock pools, puppets and, of course, lashings of glorious *gelato* (ice cream) should ensure no dull moments for youngsters. Added to that, the Sicilians are no exception to the Italian rule that they adore children and welcome them with open arms just about everywhere. START: **Mt. Etna.** Trip length: 7–10 days.

① Mt. Etna. The best place to start to get up close to A Muntagna ('the mountain' in local dialect) is the Rifugio Sapienza at Etna Sud from where you take a ride on the Funvia dell'Etna (Etna cable car) up to 2,500m (8,202ft). The ride in the little cabins teetering over mounds of lava is usually a great hit with children. From Monte Montagnola (at 2,500m/8,202ft) it's possible (weather and volcanic activity permitting) to walk up to the crater area at 2,920m (9,580ft), which takes around 4 hours return. If this is likely to be too energetic for little ones, special 4x4 trucks with obligatory guide leave from the top of the cable car for the Bocca Nuova crater where you have a guided walk (around 45 minutes) and feel the heat of the ground. The combined ticket price for cable car plus 4x4 truck is €48. The lunar-like landscape, off-road bumps, and the sheer majesty of Etna puffing, perhaps even spitting, should make this an unforgettable experience. ⏱ ½ day. Etna cable car. ☎ 095-914141. www.funiviaetna.com. Return trip €25.50. Daily 9am–5pm and till 3:30pm in winter. For more details on walking on Etna, see p 13.

Drive south on the SP4-11, and then the SP15 following signs for Etnaland. Distance: 19km (12 miles).

② Etnaland. Etnaland is a fun-filled family day out to appeal to all ages, with a **Water Park** with 21 different attractions. The **Crocodile**

Funivia dell'Etna.

Rapids are always a big hit with youngsters, where boats ride little whirlpools, as is the 'Old Mine', infested with bats and culminating in a 'crocodile attack'. Then there are encounters with 'T-Rex' and the chance to touch the 'mammoth's' tusk in the **Dinosaur Park.** There's a children's **Lazy River** ride for little ones, laser shows, diving displays, and acrobatic feats on the trampoline. There's even a **cableway** giving panoramic views of the park and of Mt. Etna. ⏱ 2 hrs. Misterbianco-Paterno, 95032 Belpasso. ☎ 0959-897101. www.etnaland.eu/it. Admission adults €24 (€18 low season), children up to 140cm (56in) €15 (€10 low season); up to 100cm (40in) free. Daily 9am–6pm June 27–Sept 7.

Isola Bella beach, set in a cove by Taormina.

Take the SP15 following the signs for Taormina and the E45/A18. Distance: 67km (42 miles).

❸ **Taormina.** Yet another cable car ride, **Funivia** (Via Luigi Pirandello, between Taormina bus terminal and Porta Messina, daily 8am–8pm, till 1am in summer; €2 single and €3.50 return) runs down to **Lido Mazzarò,** right under Taormina. This is a great spot for sunning and bathing and just to the right of this beach is the **Isola Bella,** which is as beautiful as its name suggests. Set in a cove, the islet is lapped by bluest waters and is now a nature reserve run by the World Wildlife Fund. There's some splendid snorkeling around here and swimming off the pebbly beach. In Taormina itself, the **Teatro Greco** is a spectacular setting. Its later use as a Roman gladiatorial and wild animal arena usually draws huge interest. Above Taormina, the little hill village of **Castelmola** is a pretty spot. Its castle has frequent falconry displays from April–October (look out for fliers and billboards or contact the information centre, as below). 🕐 *1 day. Taormina tourist office, Palazzo Corvaja.* ☎ *0942-23243. www.gate2taormina.com. Teatro Greco, Via Teatro Greco.* ☎ *094-2232220. Admission €6. Daily 9am–7pm, till 4:30pm in winter.*

Drive west from Taormina on the SS185 following the signs for Gola di Alcantara, located between Francavilla and Castiglione di Sicilia. Distance: 30km (18¾ miles).

❹ **Gola di Alcantara.** The Alcantara lava gorges in the **Parco Fluviale dell'Alcántara** are the perfect spot for cooling off when the temperatures sizzle in summer. The 20m (66ft) deep gorges are carved out of the lava by the river Alcantara. You can hire waterproof trousers and wade up the gorge through the icy water—which is especially refreshing in August—although this trip is probably more suited to adventurous older children. Note that there is a risk of flash flooding in winter when entry to the gorge is forbidden. ⏰ *3 hrs. Parco Fluviale dell'Alcántara.* ☎ *0942-985010. www.parco alcantara.it. €5 for elevator down into the park. Daily.*

Drive north to join the coastal road A20 and then west following the signs to Palermo. Distance: 229km (143 miles).

⑤ Palermo Puppet Theatre. This type of theater is very popular all over Sicily. Introduced by the Spanish in the 18th century, the puppeteers usually tell the stories of Charlemagne and his chivalrous knights (Orlando and Rinaldo) against the 'villainous' Saracens. You can be sure of plenty of jousting, rowdy battles, and dragon slaying. The Museo Internazionale delle Marionette (International Puppet Museum) has 3,500 puppets from all over the world. There's a dedicated room where children can play with them or create their own, and there are regular puppet shows in the fall and winter and occasionally throughout the year. Throughout Palermo you will find several puppet theatres advertised on posters. One of the most highly acclaimed is **Mimmo Cuticchio** (Via Barra all'Olivella, 95; ☎ 091-323400; www.figlidartecuticchio.com). Set in a narrow street opposite the Teatro Massimo, this has been in the same family for generations. ⏰ *2 hrs. International Puppet Museum Via Butera, 1.* ☎ *091-328060. www. museomarionettepalermo.it. Admission adults €5, children €3. Mon–Sun 9am–1pm & Mon–Fri 3:30–6:30pm.*

⑥ Catacombe dei Cappuccini (Capuchin Catacombs). These underground catacombs, filled with around 8,000 mummified bodies of Palermitans from the 17th to the 19th centuries are a gruesome fascination for many older children. ⏰ *1 hr. Via Cappuccini,1.* ☎ *091-6524156. Admission €3, free for under-18s. Daily 8:30–1pm and 2:30–6pm.*

From Palermo, take the A29 west, take the exit signposted to Carini and right along the Via A. Vespucci for 3km (1¾ miles), look for

Marionettes at the Palermo Puppet Theatre.

the signs to Bioparco di Sicilia (half-way between Palermo and the airport).

7 **Bioparco di Sicilia.** Don't miss this dinosaur park, zoo, and playground area full of slides and tepees. There's also a bird garden, a large reptile area, a zone dedicated to L'Uomo Primitivo (primitive man), fossils and minerals, and an aquarium, plus a dedicated picnic area—a fun day out for all the family. ⏲ *2 hrs. Villagrazia di Carini, via Amerigo Vespucci, 420.* ☎ *091-8676811. www.bioparcodisicilia.it/. Admission adults €7.50, children €6; free up to 10 years. Daily 9:30–7:30pm till 5pm in fall.*

Go west along the A29 dir & SP21 signposted to Trapani/Marsala, and then the SS187 following brown signs marked 'Isole Stagnone' & Mózia. Distance: 99km (61½ miles).

8 **Le Saline & Mózia.** The coastal road between Trápani and Marsala—called the **Via del Sale** (the salt road)—is remarkable for its succession of *mulini* (windmills) and

heaps of dazzlingly white salt drying in the sun. The **Museo Saline Ettore e Inferza** (opposite the pier for Mózia) has a good selection of local foods and crafts and the guided tours give an insight into the salt-making process and why the salt from here is reputedly the best in Italy. From the quay take the little ferry boat to the tiny island of **Mózia (Motya)** (see p 52). This is a lovely spot for a picnic among the remains of this ancient Phoenician town, while spotting ducks, herons, and all kinds of water birds that congregate to the shallow, warm waters of these wetlands, known as the **Riserva Naturale di Stagnone**. ⏲ *2-3 hrs. Museo Saline Ettore e Inferza.* ☎ *0923-966936. Free admission, guided tours €4. Daily Apr–Oct 9am–6:30pm.*

Tip

Salina is a local specialty for costume jewelry, made with salt and flour paste, allowed to harden, and then colored with paint: inexpensive, yet pretty. ●

Saltpans near Mózia.

4 The Great Outdoors

Best **Beaches**

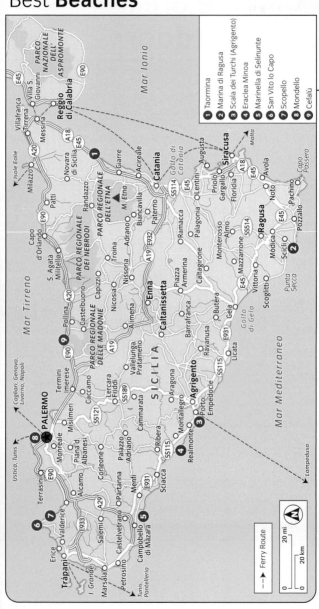

1 Taormina
2 Marina di Ragusa
3 Scala dei Turchi (Agrigento)
4 Eraclea Minoa
5 Marinella di Selinunte
6 San Vito lo Capo
7 Scopello
8 Mondello
9 Cefalù

--▸ Ferry Route

0   20 mi
0   20 km

Crescents of golden sand, pebbly beaches backed by towering cliffs, tiny coves, and black lava rocks—all dipping into dazzling shades of aquamarine seas—there's a beach for everyone in Sicily. This chapter contains a sprinkling of ideas, but as a general rule the longest, sandiest beaches are on the western coast. Don't forget the designer sunglasses—as indispensable to Sicilians as the beach itself.

Tip

Off-season, beaches tend to look very neglected, but a transformation takes place at Easter. The lidos have sun-loungers, parasols, and usually showers and restrooms, for which you pay. Other public beaches are free but often lacking in facilities, and so go prepared with sunhat, sunscreen, and plenty of water.

❶ Taormina. Taormina has no beach itself, but below the town you have a choice between the nearby pebbly inlets of **Mazzarò** and, a few kilometers to the south, the sands of **Giardini-Naxos.**

Mazzarò has a couple of pebbly beaches, as well as grottoes and coves that beg to be explored. They are easily accessible by *funivia* (cable car) from Via Luigi Pirandello in Taormina. The southernmost of the two beaches is the more crowded

with plenty of watersports on offer and facilities such as parasols, sun-loungers, and showers. My favorite here is **Lido La Pigna** (Via Nazionale Mazzaro: daily admission €10 including parasol, sun-lounger, and facilities: banana boat rides and water skiing at extra charge). Between the two beaches, the tiny islet of **Isola Bella** is the most famous and spectacular beach in the bay of Taormina (see Chapter 3, p 64).

Just 5km (3 miles) south of Taormina, the beach of **Giardini Naxos** is the longest one in the region. The fine and coarse sands are divided into two parts—*spiaggia libera* (free beach) and various lidos, where you pay for your sun-beds, shades, and watersports. The promenade is full of cafés, bars, and restaurants and this is a very popular resort for Italian families and package tours, especially during July and August.

View over the bay at Taormina.

Marina di Ragusa.

② Marina di Ragusa. Although the beaches are virtually deserted out of season, Marina di Ragusa remains perennially popular—especially with Italians and Germans—mainly due to the TV series *Il Commissario Montalbano*. Adapted from the novels by Andrea Camilleri, the series charts the life and times of the fractious, fictional Sicilian detective Montalbano at his seaside villa in *Marinella*—in reality Marina di Ragusa. The main allure of this bustling resort is the long, sandy beach—arguably the best in the area—and some fine fish restaurants and bars along the promenade. A 16th-century watchtower stands sentinel over the swathe of sand, where you will find private lidos as well as free beaches and good opportunities for windsurfing and other watersports.

③ Scala dei Turchi (Agrigento). Dazzlingly white cliffs made of soft clay and limestone lead like a staircase (*scala*) down to two fine sandy beaches here. Locals will tell you that this area was where Arab and Turkish pirates took refuge during storms or used it as a safe haven during battles with the Saracens. Still largely off the tourist radar, it's one of the island's most spectacular sites—especially at sunset and the perfect spot for a languorous picnic or a fishy feast at the **Lido Scala dei Turchi** (☎ **0922-814563**) above the beach. To get there from Agrigento, drive southwest to Porto Empedocle, and then west following signs for Realmonte. Distance: 15km (9 miles) from Agrigento.

④ Eraclea Minoa. Midway between **Agrigento** and **Selinunte** are the ruins of the ancient Greek city Eraclea Minoa perched on a white sandstone headland overlooking a wide, sandy beach. Out of season, you can have this picturesque spot pretty much to yourself, but come July and August the sands heave with bronzing bodies and you need to arrive early even to get a parking space. There are a couple of bars and restaurants on the beach, and sun-loungers and parasols for hire. If *fango* (mud) is your idea of beauty heaven, head for the western end of the beach to join the locals in smearing the greenish slime off the rock onto your skin and bake in the sun for a few minutes. It is supposed to have great therapeutic effects and is utterly free—just don't forget to wash it off. To get there from Agrigento, take the SS115 northwest and follow the brown signs to the

Eraclea Minoa archeological site and then carry straight down the twisting road for a couple of kilometers until you see the sign for Lido Garibaldi. The journey is 37km (23 miles) from Agrigento.

⑤ Marinella di Selinunte. From the romantic ruins of Selinunte, gaze down onto the long, sandy crescent of Marinella—a fishing village that has grown into a popular seaside resort. Sometimes the seaweed here can be a nuisance, in which case head about 10 minutes east of the port, to **Mare Pineta beach**—framed as its name suggests by fragrant pine trees.

⑥ San Vito lo Capo. The main appeal of this lively resort of white cube-shaped houses festooned with bougainvillea is the wide, soft sands set on a promontory on the northwestern tip of the island. Sometimes pinkish at other times pearly-white, the colors change to reflect the time of day, but at all times they are spectacular, backed by jagged cliffs that plummet into crystalline seas.

Tip

For six days in late September, San Vito lo Capo celebrates its traditional, celebrated dish—fish couscous in the Cous Cous Fest (www.couscousfest. it). There are free samplings, nightly concerts in Piazza Santuario, and a spectacular fireworks display at midnight on the last night.

⑦ Scopello. Once devoted to tuna fishing, the *tonnara* (tuna fishery buildings) here have been out of use since the 1980s, but visitors still come to enjoy its idyllic cove. The location for scenes from the movie *Ocean's Twelve*, the cove is remarkable for the *faraglioni* (rock towers) rising from seas in every hue of swimming-pool blue. The little beach at **Tonnara di Scopello** is shingly, and the waters clear. The main beach—**Baia di Guidaloca**—is also pebbly and sheltered for swimming. Scopello is also the southern entrance to the **Riserva Naturale dello Zingaro**—Sicily's first nature reserve covering 7km (4½ miles) of unspoiled coastline, with secluded coves of white-pebble beaches accessible only on foot. My favorites are **Capreria, Marinella,** and **Uzzo** (respectively 1km (½ mile), 3km (1½ miles), and 7km (4½ miles) along the tracks). ☎ *0924-35108/800-116616, www.*

Marinella di Selinunte.

Enjoy Cefalù's beach scene.

riservazingaro.it. Admission €3. Open daily summer 7am–8pm, winter 8am–4pm.

Tip

To explore the underwater paradise of the Zingaro nature reserve, take a tour or dive from Tonnara di Scopello with the Cetaria Diving Center. There are courses for first-timers and several wrecks and underwater grottoes for experienced divers to explore. ☎ *0924-541073. www. cetaria.com.*

⑧ Mondello. Only 11km (7 miles) from the capital, this is where city dwellers come for a bit of Palermo-by-the-sea action. The crescent-shaped sandy beach follows the lee of **Monte Pellegrino** for two kilometers, dominated by a vast Art Nouveau pier in the center. Some stretches of beach are private (where you pay for your sun-lounger and shade), but others are public

(free), and there's plenty to amuse water babes as well as sun worshippers. In high summer it's packed with Palermitan teenagers who like their beaches sociable. The evening *passeggiata*—where everyone struts to see and be seen—is among Sicily's finest, and later open-air discos crank up the volume. There are quieter resorts west around the headland at **Sferracavallo, Isola delle Femmine,** and **Terrasini.**

⑨ Cefalù. Families flock to Cefalu's 1½km (1-mile) long beach—one of Sicily's best—to swim in the turquoise, shallow, clear water and bask on the golden sands. Opposite the harbor, about 20 minutes' walk from the old town, **Caldura beach** is relatively day-tripper free and has none of the lido trappings; therefore it offers a welcome alternative to the main beach in high season. About 7km (4½ miles) towards Palermo, the long sandy beach of **Le Salinelle** is especially popular with windsurfers. ●

Western Sicily

1 Bagheria
2 Palermo
3 Monreale
4 Segesta
5 Trapani
6 Erice
7 Mózia
8 Marsala
9 Mazara del Vallo
10 Selinunte

Where to Stay & Dine
Al Ristorante Pierrot 11
Hotel Alceste 12
Kempinski Hotel 13
La Bettola dal 1972 14
Taverna del Pavone 15

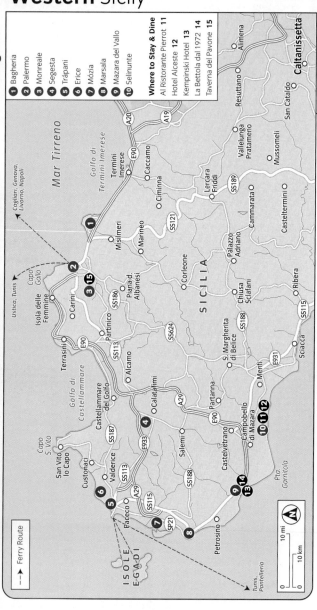

Ferry Route

The western side of Sicily is made up of more than just the capital, **Palermo**—although this is reason enough to linger. Much of Sicilian history was shaped around here with fantastic temples and the ruins of the former civilizations of Sicily's invaders. Sometimes you feel that you could be in North Africa, especially around Trápani and Mazara del Vallo; at other times you will be assailed by stories of Mafia activity. But throughout the region, you can be pretty much assured of gourmet delights and splendid wines.
START: **Bagheria. Trip Length 7–10 days.**

A Note on Hotels & Restaurants

For a full list, see Chapter 6: in Palermo, p 130; in Erice, p 152; in Marsala, p 156.

❶ **Bagheria.** Set on the southern slopes of **Monte Catalfano**, just east of Palermo, **Bagheria** was the summer refuge of the 18th- and 19th-century nobility, who came here to escape the sizzling heat. At that time it was an idyll of vineyards, olive groves, and citrus fruits. Now the countryside is largely gashed by factories and ugly modern buildings and, in the late 20th century, it was rumored to be a hotbed of Mafia activity. But those vestiges of former nobility remain in a series of decaying, yet still beautiful, Baroque villas. The utterly bizarre **Villa Palagonia** is known as the 'Villa of Monsters'. It was decorated by the hunchbacked Ferdinando Gravina Alliata, grandson of the Prince of Palagonia, whose mind, clearly as contorted as his back, led him to order frightening caricatures of his wife's lovers in the form of 200 statues adorning the wall in front of the façade. Goethe described the hideous figures as 'beggars of both sexes, men and women of Spain, Moors, Turks, hunchbacks, deformed persons of every kind, dwarfs, musicians, Pulcinellas.' Sixty-four of the original statues

remain perched malevolently around the garden. Inside, the hunchback demonstrated more eccentric behavior by hiding spikes under apparently comfortable velvet seats and mirrors that distorted the figures of visitors into grotesque shapes.

In pleasant contrast, antique meets modern in the Baroque **Villa Cattólica**, completed in 1736 by Giuseppe Bonanni Filangeri, Prince of Cattólica. Now it contains the **Gallería Comunale d'Arte Moderna e Contempóraneo** with a permanent exhibition of the works by Sicily's best-known modern

Monsterous statue at the bizarre Villa Palagonia, Bagheria.

artist, and Bagheria's most famous son, Renato Guttuso (1912–87). Staunchly anti-Fascist and later anti-Mafia, Guttuso's use of color and daringly decisive lines are arrestingly sensuous. His tomb is in the garden, designed by his sculptor friend, Giacomo Manzù—a surreal 'blue capsule' set amidst citrus trees and cacti. ⏱ *2 hrs. Tourist information office, Corso Umberto, 171 (close to Villa Palagonia).* ☎ *091-909020. Admission €5. Tues & Fri 5–7pm. Villa Palagonia, Piazza Garibaldi.* ☎ *091-932088. www. villapalagonia.it. Daily 9am–1pm & 4–7pm; till 5:30pm in winter. Villa Cattólica, Via Consolare, 9.* ☎ *091-943902. Tues–Sun 9am–6pm.*

From Bagheria, take the coastal road SS113 to Palermo. Distance: 14km (8¾ miles)

❷ **Palermo.** Shabby yet chic and seductively shady, this is a tantalizing city full of contrasts, all in a stupendous setting. Try to allow three days. *For a full list of attractions, see Chapters 2 (p 17) and 6 (p 122).*

From Palermo, drive from Porta Nuova on the Corso Calatafimi to Monreale. Or take the bus no. 389 from Piazza Indipendenza in Palermo for the 40 minute trip. **Distance: 10km (6 miles) south-west of Palermo.**

❸ **Monreale.** This hilltop town, 'Royal Mountain', counts among the top attractions of southern Italy, thanks to its superlative **Cattedrale di Monreale** (Piazza Duomo/ Piazza Guglielmo il Buono, ☎ **091-6404413**), which contains some of the world's most beautiful medieval mosaics. Unmissable, too, are the cloisters, **Chiostro dei Benedettini,** representing the flowering of Islamic architecture—often referred to as a 'preview of Paradise' by Sicilians. *For more information, see p 57.*

From Monreale, drive southwest on the SS186, and then the A29 & A29 dir signposted to Segesta. Distance: 59km (37 miles).

❹ **Segesta.** Standing proud on a hill overlooking a deep ravine, the ★★★ Temple of Segesta (☎ **0924-952356**; daily 9am–7pm, till 4pm in winter) is one of the world's most perfectly preserved survivors of antiquity. Built in the 5th century BC and supported by 36 Doric columns, it was left unfinished, probably due to warfare with Segesta's great enemy, **Selinunte.** Framed by mountains and glowing gold in the afternoon Sicilian

Island Cycling

Favignana, the main island of the Isole Egadi (Egadis), is virtually flat on the eastern side and ideal for cycling around. The only high point of this butterfly-shaped isle is **Monte Caterina** (302m/ 991ft) on the western side. You'll find cycle hire shops dotted throughout the island, especially at Favignana harbor, and so it's not necessary to transport one across from the mainland. You can easily see the whole of Favignana in an afternoon, but take time for at least one dip in one of the many coves, such as **Cala Rossa** (Red Cove) where you can swim off the rocks in turquoise, crystalline waters.

Cloisters, Cattedrale di Monreale.

sun, this is perhaps the most magnificent of all views in Sicily. *For more information, see Chapter 3, p 51.*

From Segesta, take the SP57 and then A29 dir west signposted Trápani. Distance: 40km (25 miles).

⑤ Trápani. Bordered on either side by the sea, Trápani is the capital of its eponymous province, the most westerly region in Sicily, covering an area of great natural beauty. Once a Phoenician outpost, today it has a fine historic core with a maze of narrow streets and Baroque mansions that are well worth a stroll around. Yet many tourists overlook these in favor of the nearby medieval hill town of **Erice** (see ⑥ below) or as a jumping-off point for the **Egadi islands** (see p 46).

From Trápani, take the Via Fardella to the end of the street and you'll see signs pointing to Erice, following the A29, northeast of Trápani. It's a very twisty drive of around 30 minutes. Distance: 14km (8¾ miles). An

alternative is to take the *funivia* (cable car) up from the base station at Via Caserta, Trápani— which takes less than 15 minutes, but doesn't run on windy or very misty days.

The Doric columns of the Temple of Segesta.

Windmill, Mozia.

6 Erice. The mountaintop setting, with the whole of the west coast laid out before you and, on a clear day, vistas right across to Tunisia, are testimony enough to Erice's popularity. What's more, the village itself is enchanting with its medieval cobbled streets adorned with Baroque balconies and flower-filled

View from hilltop over the sea at Erice.

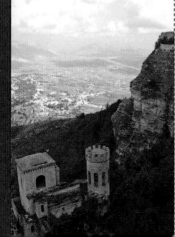

courtyards. Back in the mists of time it was also a shrine to Venus, the goddess of love, whose temple was a famous landmark and mentioned by the Roman poet, Virgil. *For more information see Chapters 2 (p 19) and 6 (p 150)*.

From Erice, take the SP3, and then the A29 dir heading towards A29/Palermo/Mazara del Vallo, exit on the SP21 Strada Provinciale Trápani-Marsala and follow the brown signs for Isole Stagnone and ferry sign for Mózia, 'imbarco per Mózia'. Distance: 40km (25 miles).

7 Mózia. Framed by dazzling white saltpans and windmills, this ancient Phoenician site seems to float on its little island in the Stagnone wetlands reserve. It lay undisturbed for centuries until 1913, when James Whitaker, an amateur archeologist and Marsala wine magnate, rediscovered it. Now it's the world's best-preserved Phoenician site and the museum holds some of the finest of Sicily's Greek statues.

For more information, see Chapter 3, p 52.

From the embarkment stage for Mózia, head south on the SP21 to Marsala. Distance: 11km (6¾ miles).

8 Marsala. Set on the western-most tip of Sicily on **Cape Boeo**, this is a thriving town steeped in history with plenty of elegant buildings and a North African flavor to its labyrinthine alleys and narrow streets. Also steeped in the wine that has made the town world-famous, it would be sacrilege not to indulge in some tastings. *See Chapter 6, p 154 for more information.*

From Marsala, head southwest on the SS115 to Mazara del Vallo. Distance: 23 km (14½ miles)

9 Mazara del Vallo. Very Moorish in character, this waterfront town's nucleus is **La Casbah**—a tangle of little alleyways that were once the heart of the Saracen city. Even today it has a large Maghreb population made up of many hundreds who come to work on

Mazara's big fishing fleet, where tuna is king.

Count Roger's Norman **Castello** is spectacularly floodlit at night and from here it's a short stroll to the Baroque **Duomo** (Piazza della Repubblica). But the town's highlight is the ★★★ **Museo del Satiro** with its prized bronze statue **Il Satiro Danzante** (the Dancing Satyr). This 4th century BC statue was discovered by fishermen 40km (25 miles) off the shores of Tunisia. First they unknowingly trawled in the bronze leg and, spellbound, continued to fish in the area over a period of time in the hope of re-uniting it with the rest of the statue. Their patience was finally rewarded and in 1998 the torso of the satyr was brought to the surface. An excellent video tells the story of the find (in Italian with English subtitles) and the subsequent painstaking restoration of this beautiful bacchanalian satyr, dancing ecstatically, his hair streaming back. Sadly, photos are forbidden—but the movement and beauty of this bronze treasure should remain etched in your memory.

Façade of the Baroque Duomo, Mazara del Vallo.

Temple ruins at Selinunte.

🕐 *1 hr. Tourist Information: Piazza S. Veneranda, 2.* ☎ *0923-941727. www.apt.Trápani.it. Mon–Sat 8am–2:15pm Sun 9am–noon. Museo del Satiro, Piazza Plebiscito.* ☎ *0923-933917. Admission €6. Tues–Sat 9am–7pm, Sun 9am–1pm.*

From Mazara del Vallo, head south on the SS115 to Selinunte. Distance: 24km (15 miles).

🔟 **Selinunte.** In the 7th century BC, this was a walled city adorned with magnificent Greek temples. The French author Guy de Maupassant (1885) called it 'an immense heap of fallen columns, now aligned and placed side by side on the ground like dead soldiers, having fallen in a chaotic manner'. Yet the **Doric Temple E** is a splendid sight and the most complete of all, while the **Acropolis** contains the ruins of the five **West Temples,** as well as sections of well-preserved walls and city streets. *For more information, see Chapter 3, p 53.*

Where to **Stay & Dine**

★ **Al Ristorante Pierrot** MARI-NELLA DI SELINUNTE Seafood and fish are the staples here with a terrace opening out onto the Mediterranean. The catches of the day are as popular as the fish couscous that regularly appears on the menu. It also serves a very good buffet. *Via Marco Polo, 108.* ☎ *0924-46205. Reservations recommended. Menus €25–30. AE, DC, MC, V. Lunch & dinner daily.*

Hotel Alceste SELINUNTE, MARI-NELLA Within walking distance of the archeological park (about 15 minutes), this is a small family-run hotel with neat rooms and compact, tiled bathrooms. The restaurant serves tasty Sicilian cuisine. *Via*

Alceste, 21, Marinella di Selinunte.
☎ *0924-46184. www.hotelalceste.it.*
30 units. Doubles €70–90. AE, DC,
MC, V.

★★★ **Kempinski Hotel** GIARDINO
DI CONSTANZA, MAZARA DEL
VALLO   Lying in its own grounds
outside Mazara, this hotel is an oasis
of calm in elegant surroundings.
Resembling a low flat-roofed manor
house with crenellated towers, it's
set among palms, vineyards, and
olive groves. All rooms have balconies or terraces and are beautifully
appointed, some taking their inspiration from Moorish décor, others with
lofty ceilings decorated in warm colors with wide gilt-framed mirrors.
The gardens are fountain-splashed
and adorned with gazebos and flowers. There are swimming pools, tennis courts, a spa, and a Beach Club.
The Kempinski is the first five-star
resort in this part of Sicily. *Via
Salemi,* ☎ *0923-675000. www.*

*kempinski-sicily.com. 91 units. Dou-
bles €447–523. AE, MC, V.*

★ **La Bettola dal 1972** MAZARA
DEL VALLO   This top fish and
seafood restaurant is presided over
by the chef/patron Pietro Sardo,
who personally suggests and pre-
pares your feast. It's very popular
with the locals, and the extensive
wine list includes more than 200
Sicilian wines. *Via F. Maccagnone,
32.* ☎ *0923-946422. www.ristorante
labettola.it. Menus €25–45. MC, V.
Closed Wed.*

★ **Taverna del Pavone** MONRE-
ALE   Just a few steps uphill from
the cathedral, this welcoming family-run, rustic tavern specializes in
good Sicilian food. The pasta is
home-made—try the *maccheroni*
(macaroni) with local country
cheese. *Vicolo Pensato, 18.* ☎ *091-
6406209. www.tavernadelpavone.
eu. Menus €25–32. AE, DC, MC, V.
Closed Mon and 15–30th June.*

Swimming pool at the Kempinski Hotel, Mazara del Vallo.

North East Sicily

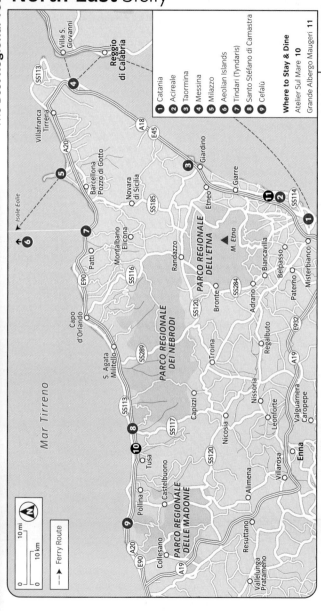

Mar Tirreno

Isole Eolie

PARCO REGIONALE DEI NEBRODI

PARCO REGIONALE DELL'ETNA

M. Etna

PARCO REGIONALE DELLE MADONIE

Enna

Reggio di Calabria

Villa S. Giovanni

Villafranca Tirrena

Barcellona Pozzo di Gotto

Novara di Sicilia

Giardino

Giarre

Etneo

Biancavilla

Belpasso

Paternò

Misterbianco

Montalbano Elicona

Patti

Randazzo

Bronte

Adrano

Regalbuto

Capo d'Orlando

S. Agata Militello

Capizzi

Troina

Nicosia

Nissoria

Leonforte

Valguarnera Caropepe

Villarosa

Tusa

Castelbuono

Alimena

Resuttano

Pollina

Collesano

Vallelunga Pratameno

Ferry Route

0   10 mi

0   10 km

The eastern coast is dominated by Mt. Etna, Europe's highest volcano. Majestic, brooding, and constantly threatening to blow her top, the volcanic peak provides the most dramatic of backdrops, especially for Taormina's Greek Theater. There are Greek remains, too, at Tyndaris, and Aeolus, Greek god of winds, gave his name to the spectacular volcanic Aeolian Islands.

1 Catania. This lava city is the capital of the eastern part of Sicily—and the second largest city after Palermo. As well as boasting some of Europe's richest repositories of the Baroque, it's also a lively town. Maybe the omnipresent **Mt. Etna** makes everyone want to *carpe diem* (seize the day)—because the volcano has spewed its lava forth on countless occasions. *For more information, see Chapters 2 (p 14), 3 (p 58), and 6 (p 106). For listings, see Chapter 6.*

From Catania, drive north on the coast road, the SS114 to Acireale. Distance: 17½km (11 miles).

2 Acireale. This small coastal town, surrounded by lemon groves, is largely off the tourist radar—but undeservedly so. Like Catania, much damage was done to Acireale in the earthquake of 1693 and, like the big city, it has splendid Baroque architecture. Since Greek and certainly Roman times, it has been a popular **spa center** with the sulfur-rich Etna volcanic waters as the magnet. There are plenty of sulfur baths—check with the tourist office (see below) for a selection. The central square, the **Piazza Duomo**, is dominated by the tall spires of the 16th-century **Duomo**. Just beyond is Piazza Vigo and the **Basilica di San Sebastiano** (☎ 095-601313)—one of Sicily's finest examples of Baroque architecture. Other gems are the **Chiesa di San Domenico** (Piazza San Domenico) and the **Palazzo Musmeci**—with its graceful balconies and rococo windows. The town is also famous for its puppet theater and its *Carnevale* (carnival) celebrations—among the island's most showy—for five fun-filled days in Feb/Mar. ⏱ *2 hrs. Tourist information, Via Scionti, 15. ☎ 095-891999, www.acirealeturismo.it. Duomo, Piazza Duomo. ☎ 095-601797. Daily 8am–noon and 4–7pm.*

Lemon groves surround the town of Acireale.

Riviera Dei Ciclopi

The coast around here is known as 'the Riviera of the Cyclops' and just south of Acireale is the fishing village **Aci Trezza**, famous for its jagged basalt rocks, the **Scogli dei Ciclopi**, that tower from the sea depths. Legend says that they were thrown by the blinded Cyclops (who is rumored to live in Mt. Etna) at the fleeing Odysseus.

From Acireale, drive north following signs to A18/E45 signposted to Taormina. Distance: 41½km (26 miles).

❸ ★★★ Taormina. Perched on **Monte Tauro** high above the azure sea with Etna in the background, this is the most beautiful town in Sicily—but as a victim of its success can be overcrowded. But to miss it would be to deprive yourself of a real treat. Try to visit out of season, and be sure to see the **Teatro Greco** (see p 64). *For more information see Chapter 6, p 142.*

Teatro Greco, Taormina.

Tip

By car, driving along the Corso Umberto, Taormina's main drag, is impossible. The main car park, Parcheggio Lumbi (Contrada Lumbi, signposted off the Taormina Nord Autostrada) is expensive at around €25 per 24 hours. Mazzarò Parking (Via Nazionale, near the cable car station) is slightly cheaper. Or choose a hotel either with its own parking or one farther down the hill.

From Taormina, take the A18/E45 north, and then the A20 following the signs for Messina. Distance: 52km (32½ miles).

❹ Messina. It may be the most modern city on the island and it may also be largely a tacky industrial port, but spare a thought for its misfortunes over the centuries. You may be surprised to learn that Messina was the setting for Shakespeare's *Much Ado About Nothing* and it has some appealing sights at its heart.

Over the centuries, Messina has been razed to the ground by earthquakes, most recently in 1908, which claimed the lives of over 80,000 people and sank the coast by half a meter. No sooner had the city been rebuilt than it was flattened again, by Allied bombers in World War II—the most heavily bombed of any town in the whole of Italy. Yet its origins go back to the 8th century BC when it was known by the Ancient Greeks as

The restored Norman Duomo at Messina.

Zancle (sickle) after the shape of its harbor and splendid position overlooking the straits to mainland Italy. Don't miss the painstakingly restored Norman ★ **Duomo** with its 15th century carvings depicting Sicilian agrarian life on the central doorway, the valuable reliquaries in the **Tesoro**, and the highlight, the **Manta d'Oro** (golden mantle)—a special cover for the picture of *La Madonna della Lettera* that sits on the altar. The *campanile* (bell tower) houses one of the world's largest astronomical clocks, built in Strasbourg in 1733. Noon is showtime when a lion (Messina's ancient emblem) roars, a cock crows—and much more besides.

North of the Duomo, the ★★ **Museo Regionale** is one of Sicily's greatest provincial museums with a splendid collection of art from the 15–17th centuries. ⏲ *2 hrs. Tourist information Via Calabria, 301.* ☎ *090 640221. www.provincia.messina.it. Mon–Thur 9am-1:30pm and 3pm-5pm; Fri 9pm-1:30pm. Duomo, Piazza del Duomo. Mon–Sat 8am–6pm, Sun 7:30am–1pm and 4–7:30pm. Museo Regionale, Viale della Libertà, 465.*

☎ *090-361292. Mon–Sat 9am–1:30pm and Tues, Thurs, Sat 3–5:30pm, Sun 9am–12:30pm).*

From Messina, take the A20 to Milazzo. Distance: 39km (24¼ miles).

⑤ **Milazzo.** Milazzo's chief allure is as the embarkation point for the **Aeolian Islands** (see ⑥ below). However, the port has an attractive Spanish quarter tucked away in the lee of the imposing huge **Castello** (guided tours hourly Tues–Sun), built originally by Frederick II in 1239, and later enlarged by Charles V. Access to the castle is by the **Salita Castello**, which takes you through the Spanish quarter. ⏲ *1 hr. Tourist information: Piazza C Duilio, 10.* ☎ *090-9222865. Mon–Fri 8am–2pm and 4–7pm, Sat 8am–2pm.*

⑥ **Aeolian Islands.** The sailors of Ancient Greek times believed these seven islands to be the home of Aeolus, god of the winds. The winds were kept in one of the Aeolian's caves and famously were given to Odysseus in a bag to be opened

The port and imposing castello at Milazzo.

only with great caution. But curiosity got the better of the crew, who opened the bag only to have the ship blown straight back into port. At times, all those winds of the world do seem to converge here, but hydrofoils and ferries permitting, visitors arrive in their droves, smitten by the natural beauty of these volcanic isles. *For more information see Chapters 2 (p 26) and 3 (p 43).*

From Milazzo to Tindari, take the A20 going west, the SS113, and then turn right at the SP107. Distance: 35km (21¾ miles).

7 Tíndari (Tyndaris). One of Sicily's last Greek settlements—the ruins of **Tyndaris** (Capo Tíndari; ☎ 0941-369023; daily 9am–1 hr before sunset)—lie hidden amidst cypress and olive trees and prickly pears on a lonely rocky promontory. Founded by Dionysius the Elder in 396 BC, this was one of Sicily's last Greek settlements. Most of the ruins visible today date from Roman times, including the **basilica** and the **Roman villa**, which still has the original floor mosaics. There is also a 4th century BC **Teatro Greco**, sculpted into the hillside. Although the remains may be small, the sweeping coastal views are to sigh for. *For more information, see Chapter 3, p 55.*

From Tyndaris, drive west on the SP118, and then the A20, SS117, & SS113 to Santo Stefano di Camastra. Distance: 80km (50 miles).

8 Santo Stéfano di Camastra. Lying at the western end of the **Parco Regionale dei Nebrodi** and the eastern end of the **Parco Regionale delle Madonie** (see Chapter 3,

Bridge of Size

The dream of building a bridge across the 3¼km (2-mile) Messina Straits may finally become reality. It would be the world's longest suspension bridge, with pylons as high as New York's Empire State Building, and would need to handle some 5,000 cars an hour as well as high-speed trains. Both seismologists and environmentalists are in opposition, but following the re-election of Silvio Berlusconi as Prime Minister and his strong belief that it will create thousands of jobs, boost tourism, and improve transport links between the 'toe' of Italy and Sicily, work could begin late in 2009. It remains to be seen how the construction contracts between the Sicilian and Calabrian Mafia will be divvied up.

p 36), the coastal town of Santo Stéfano is famous for its ceramics. The area is said to have some of the best clay in Sicily and on the approach roads you'll see plenty of vendors hawking their wares. Before parting with your euros, visit the **Museo Civico delle Ceramiche** for an insight into the manufacturing process. Of the many shops in town, the family-run business **Ceramiche Franco** (Via Nazionale, 8; ☎ 0921-3377222) is a good option, renowned for its craftsmanship. 🕐 1 hr. Tourist information: Museo Civico delle Ceramiche, Palazzo Trabia, Via Palazzo. ☎ 0921-331110. Tues–Sun 9am–1pm and 4–8pm, reduced opening in winter.

From Santo Stéfano, drive west on the SS113, then A20/E90, and then the SS113 signposted Cefalù. Distance: 42km (26 miles).

Santo Stéfano is famous for its ceramics.

9 Cefalù. Pretty as a picture, the charming beach resort of Cefalù was among the star locations in the Oscar-winning film *Cinema Paradiso*. Inevitably, it gets very crowded during high season with the 'fly and flop' brigade who come for the sandy beaches (see Chapter 4, p 72), shopping, and buzzing nightlife. *For more information, see Chapter 6, p 112.*

Where to **Stay & Dine**

Tip

In addition to hotels in Catania, Taormina, the Aeolian Islands, and Cefalù, the following also make good bases.

★ **Atelier Sul Mare** CASTEL DI TUSA 'Have you ever slept *in* an art work?' This is the question posed by this art hotel's owner, Messina-born Antonio Presti. Now is your chance in this most unusual hotel where 15 of the rooms have been decorated by different artists. Choose perhaps between The Nest, Earth and Fire, or the Mouth of Truth—or you could stay in a different artistic installation each night, if the hotel isn't full. Another 25 rooms are 'conventional' but with artistic flair. *Via Cesare Battisti, 4 (8km (5 miles) west of Santo Stéfano di Camastra).* ☎ *0921-334295. www.ateliersulmare.it. 40 units. Doubles (conventional) €120–170; doubles (designer/art) €160–230. DC, MC, V.*

★★ **Grande Albergo Maugeri** ACIREALE Located in the center of town, this four star traditional hotel has been recently renovated to a high standard with smart, modern bathrooms. There is a 'Well Being' center and a good restaurant serving typical island cuisine. *Piazza Garibaldi, 27.* ☎ *095-608686. www. hotel-maugeri.it. 59 units. Doubles €90–200. AE, DC, MC, V.*

South West Sicily

1 Corleone
2 Caltabellotta
3 Sciacca
4 Agrigento
5 Caltanissetta
6 Enna
7 Morgantina
8 Villa Romana del Casale

Where to Stay & Dine

Colleverde Park Hotel 9
Grand Hotel Mosè 10
Leon d'Oro 11
Mosaici-da Battiato 12
Rocco Forte Verdura Golf &
  Spa Resort 13
Trattoria dei Templi 14
Trattoria La Ruota 15

The highlights of southwest Sicily are the temples of Agri-gento and the mosaics at the Villa Romana. But there are many other treasures in store in the unspoiled interior where little farming villages stand isolated on their hilltops, as if in a time warp. Begin your tour in Il Corleonese—the central area known as much for its fertile land as for Corleone, hometown of the Mafia.

1 **Corleone.** Infamous as the cra-dle of the Mafia, the town's setting in an upland bowl, dominated by two rocky outcrops with a lovely his-toric core belies its notorious reputation. The name of the central piazza may have been changed to Falcone-Borsellino, in honor of the slaughtered anti-Mafia magistrates, but all seems quite peaceful today. Between 1944 and 1948, Corleone had one of the world's highest mur-der rates with 153 violent deaths perpetrated. It was from here, too, that Mafia boss Toto Riina ruled

before going into hiding till his arrest in 1993. Other members of the Corleonese clan include Ber-nardo Provenzano who was finally captured in 2006 with the blood of many on his hands, including Fal-cone and Borsellino. Although Mario Puzo's choice of Don Corleone as the name in *The Godfather* was pretty accurate, the movies were not shot here because the town was too developed for director Francis Ford Coppola's eye. Instead the Sicilian scenes were filmed in Sáv-oca (see Chapter 6 for Taormina excursions). Do visit the Mafia Museum, or more correctly, the **Museo Anti-Mafia** (Via Orfanotrofio, 7 open: Mon–Sat 8:30am–1pm and 3:30–7:30pm, and Sun am). On view are graphic photographs of the aftermath of the Mafia killings in the early 1980s and shots illustrating the violent history of the Cosa Nostra. 🕐 *1 hr. Tourist information: Museo Anti-Mafia, Via Orfanotrofio, 7. Admission free. Mon–Sat 8:30am–1pm and 3:30–7:30pm, Sun am.*

From Corleone, for the twisting route south to Caltabellotta, take the SP80, and then turn right onto the SS188, followed by the SS386, then right onto the SP37. Distance: 46km (28¾ miles).

② **Caltabellotta.** This tiny mountain village (950m/3,117ft high) is exquisite. The ruins of the Norman *castello* (open at all times) perch on the highest point, the place where the heir to the Norman throne, William III, was imprisoned with his mother and, in all probability, murdered by Henry VI. It was also where the peace treaty was signed between the Angevins and Aragonese that put an end to the War of the Sicilian Vespers (1302). An abandoned hermitage, **Eremo di**

The mountain village of Caltabellotta.

San Pellegrino overlooks the rugged mountainside that is sprinkled with necropoli. It's rumored that a dragon lived here on a diet of young maidens until he was killed by heroic San Pellegrino.

From Sciacca, head west to join the SP37 and continue southwest down to Sciacca. Distance: 22km (13¾ miles).

③ **Sciacca.** Taking its name from the Arabic *Xacca* (Water), this small fishing town was prized by the Arabs and before them the Phoenicians, Greeks, and Romans who all came to take the waters here. You can still bask in the sulfuric springs in the Liberty-style **Nuovo Stabilimento Termale** (Via delle Nuove Terme; ☎ 0925-961111). Walls enclose the upper town and the westernmost gate **Porta San Salvatore** leads to the main thoroughfare, **Corso Vittorio Emanuele**, and **Piazza A. Scandaliato**—an attractive spot for savoring the views with a drink. Then delve into the tangle of Moorish alleyways, peppered with ceramic shops, because this is one of Sicily's best pottery centers. It also stages one of the island's best carnivals (see The Savvy Traveler, p 157). 🕐 *2 hrs.*

Valle dei Templi, Agrigento.

From Sciacca, join the SS115 going east for about 56km (35 miles), and then exit toward Enna/Palermo on the SS189/SS640 to Agrigento. Distance: 61km (38 miles).

4 **Agrigento.** The **Valle dei Templi** and its **Archeological Museum**, a superlative example of Magna Graecia (Greater Greece), with its series of 5th century BC Doric temples (see Chapter 3, p 53), is the unmissable sight of Agrigento—unlike the views of modern Agrigento. The new quarter is among the ugliest settlements on the island. Shoddily built, often illegal buildings resulted in the disastrous landslides of 1966 that killed many people—revealing a scandal that Mafia surveyors had not checked for land subsidence and allowed their contractors to use poor quality cement. It may therefore come as a surprise to find that the core of the city is medieval. Here the atmospheric **Via Atenea** passes artisans' workshops and little alleyways full of tempting shops. Nearby is the 13th century **Abbazia di Santo Spirito** (Via Santo Spirito), with its impressive Gothic entrance, rose window, and fine stuccowork. In the adjoining convent the nuns make and sell a delicious sweet called 'kus-kus' made of pistachio nuts and chocolate. Up the hill is the originally Norman **Duomo** (Piazza Don Minzoni; ☎ 0922-490011). In contrast to the somber chapels, the choir is a Baroque romp of angels and golden garlands. And if it all gets too hot, you can escape to a beach at nearby San Leone. ⏱ *2hrs. Tourist information: Via Cesare Battisti, 15. ☎ 0922 20454. www.agrigento-sicilia.it. Open Mon–Fri 8:30am–1:30pm.*

From Agrigento, head northeast to the SS640/Strada Statale di Porto Empedocle and then the ramp to Caltanisetta. Distance: 58km (36 miles).

5 **Caltanissetta.** The route here meanders through rolling hills speckled with little villages in a wild, beautiful landscape—the rural heart of Sicily. This is by far the largest town of the interior, with all the attendant traffic problems. The huge **Duomo**

in Piazza Garibaldi contains some impressive frescoes but the town's chief claim to fame is the *digestivo* (liqueur) **Averna**—a blend of alcohol and 60 wild herbs —the leading brand of various *amari* (bitter) drinks invented by Capuchin monks in 1800. Try it at the **Vicolo Duomo** restaurant (Piazza Garibaldi, 3; ☎ 0934-582332; closed Sun and Mon lunch)—a member of the Slow Food Movement and a stylish spot for a leisurely meal. ⏱ *1–2 hrs. Tourist information: Corso Vittorio Emanuel II, 109 (just off Piazza Garibaldi).* ☎ *0934-530411. Open Mon–Fri 9am–2pm and Wed 3pm-6pm.*

From Caltanissetta, head northeast to join the A19 and take the Enna exit. Distance: 36½km (22½ miles).

❻ **Enna.** Atop a terraced mountain spur and with spectacular views, Enna has been called the 'navel of Sicily' since Ancient Greek times, vying with Caltanissetta as the geometrical center of the island. This fortress town was so well defended that, after 20 years of fruitless effort, the Arabs finally gained entrance in the year 859 by crawling through the sewers. Must-sees include the 13th century **Castello di Lombardia** (Piazza Mazzini; daily summer 8am–8pm; winter 9am–5pm) built by Frederick II, ringed with thick walls, and protected by the remaining six of the original 20 towers. **Sicilia delle Miniature** (Via Roma 533; ☎ 338-5023361) is worth a browse with its local traditions and Sicilian architecture. Look too for the Gothic **Duomo** (daily 9am–1pm and 4–7pm), built on the site of Persephone's temple in 1307, with its exuberant Baroque interior featuring huge carved columns decorated with grotesques, including snakes with human heads. Take a break in one of the cafés lining the lovely **Piazza Vittorio Emanuele** to watch the evening *passeggiata.* ⏱ *2 hrs. Tourist information: Via Roma, 413.* ☎ *0935-528228. www.apt-enna.com. Mon,Tues, Thur, Fri 8am-2pm and Wed 8am-6pm.*

Villa Romana del Casale & Piazza Armerina

Set among thickly wooded countryside, the **Villa Romana** dating from the 3rd–4th century BC has 35,000 sq m (376,737 sq ft) of world-famous mosaics—one of the highlights of any trip to Sicily. It's possible to walk or cycle from here uphill on an asphalt road to the town center of **Piazza Armerina**, 5km (3 miles) northeast. Often overlooked in favor of the Villa Romana's treasures, this is an attractive town, built on three hills. The original village dates from the 10th-century Saracen heyday, whereas the overflow town to the southeast is from the 15th-century. The old town area is centered around **Piazza Garibaldi**: there are charming, crumbling *palazzi*, a dramatically sited **Cathedral** with remarkable dome at the highest point, labyrinthine little streets to explore, and some good hotels and restaurants. Although the steep, cobbled streets make it more of a case of pushing than pedaling in town, a bike is a good way of exploring the outlying, beautiful countryside.

Mosaics at the Villa Romana del Casale near Piazza Armerina.

From Enna, drive southeast via the SP4, and then the SS561 and SS288 to Morgantina. Distance: 43km (27 miles).

❼ Morgantina. Originally settled by the Morgeti people around 1000 BC, the **Morgantina archeological site** (☎ 0935-87307; daily 9am–1 hr before sunset) is set on two hills. The main entrance is the **east hill** where a path leads to the **agora** (forum) and, on the right, a small **teatro** dating from the 3rd century BC

Piazza Armerina.

where performances are held in summer (☎ 0935-87955). *For more information, see Chapter 3, p 55.* ⏱ *1 hr.*

From Morgantina, follow the SS288 southwest to join the SS117bis and take the exit right signposted to Villa Romana del Casale. Distance: 26km (16¼ miles).

❽ ★★★ Villa Romana del Casale. One of the grandest of all Roman villas, this is Sicily's greatest Roman wonder. (For more information, see Chapter 3, p 54). The nearby little town, **Piazza Armerina**, makes for a very pleasant stopover. Built on three hills, the original village dates from the 10th-century Saracen heyday, whereas the overflow town to the southeast is 15th century. There are charming, crumbling palazzi, a dramatically sited **Cathedral** with remarkable dome, tangles of little streets to explore and some good hotels and restaurants. ⏱ *2 hrs. Tourist information: Via Umberto, 1.* ☎ *0935-687027. www.guardalasicilia.it.*

Where to **Stay & Dine**

★★ **Colleverde Park Hotel** AGRI-
GENTO   Conveniently located
between the archeological zone and
the city, with splendid views over the
Valle dei Templi, this is a favorite
hotel in Agrigento. Décor is discreetly elegant with charming art-
work, lots of exposed wood, and
large picture windows. The staff are
very helpful and the garden is a
delight, with vine-covered arbors,
terracotta terraces, and a tasteful
glass-sided restaurant. *Via Panorámica dei Templi.* ☎ *092-229555.
www.colleverdehotel.it. 53 units.
Doubles €70–170. AE, DC, MC, V.*

★ **Grand Hotel Mosè** AGRIGENTO
A modern, well-designed hotel clad
in stucco of the same honeyed tones
as the sandstone of the Valley of the
Temples. The rooms are simple yet
colorful with touches of elegant
manorial Sicilian flair. Most of the
bathrooms are shower only with tiled
floors. The free-form pool is one of
the best in town. *Viale Leonardo
Sciascia, Villaggio Mosè (3km/1¾
miles out of town).* ☎ *092-2608388.
www.iashotels.com. 96 units. Doubles €100–140. AE, DC, MC, V.*

★★ **Leon d'Oro** AGRIGENTO   At
the entrance to San Leone, this
rather unprepossessing cement-clad
modern building belies its festive
interior. For this is one of Agrigento's most fêted and popular restaurants where seafood and fish reign.
In summer you can dine outside
under a gazebo. *Via Emporium, 102,
San Leone (7km/4¼ miles south).*
☎ *0922-414400. Menus €23–50. AE,
DC, MC, V. Open Tues–Sun.*

★ **Mosaici-da Battiato** PIAZZA
ARMERINA   This simple, inexpensive countryside hotel and restaurant is ideally positioned for visiting
the famous mosaics at Villa Romana.

The restaurant specializes in home-
made traditional dishes. *Contrada
Paratore Casale, 11 (3km/1¾ miles
west).* ☎ *0935-685453. www.hotel
mosaici.com. 23 units. Doubles €50.
MC, V. Menus €18–25.*

★★★ **Rocco Forte Verdura
Golf & Spa Resort** SCIACCA
The Rocco Forte Collection opened
a brand new resort in Verdura, near
the town of Sciacca in July 2009. Set
in a 230-hectare (568-acre) estate,
one hour's drive from Palermo airport, and well placed for visiting
Agrigento and the Valley of the
Temples, it boasts impressive sea
views, six restaurants, three bars, a
golf course, infinity pool, tennis center, and a 4,000 sq m (43,056 sq ft)
state-of-the-art spa. *Verdura Golf &
Spa Resort Contrada, Verdura, Sciacca.* ☎ *0925-998180. www.rocco
fortecollection.com. 203 units. Doubles €350–720. AE, DC, MC, V.*

★ **Trattoria dei Templi** AGRI-
GENTO   Set at the bottom of the hill
between the city and Valley of the
Temples, this is a deservedly popular restaurant. Try the fresh fish,
attractively served on hand-painted
china—or such non-fishy alterna-
tives as the classic Sicilian 'pasta alla
Norma'. *Via Panorámica dei Templi,
15.* ☎ *0922-403110. Menus €25–38.
AE, DC, MC,V. Lunch and dinner
daily. Closed 30th June–10th July,
Sun July–Aug, and Fri Sep–June.*

★ **Trattoria La Ruota** PIAZZA
ARMERINA   Genuine Sicilian country fare is on the menu in this atmospheric restaurant that was formerly
a water mill. Try the specialty rabbit
with olives or homemade pork sausages. *Contrada Casale, Ouest.*
☎ *0935-680542. www.trattoriala
ruota.it. Menus €22–29. AE, MC, V.
Daily noon–3pm (lunch only).*

South Eastern Sicily

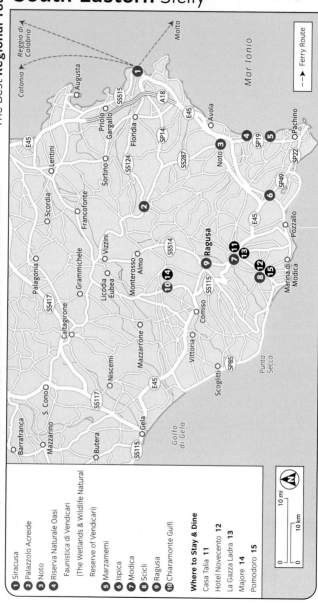

1 Siracusa
2 Palazzolo Acreide
3 Noto
4 Riserva Naturale Oasi
Faunistica di Vendicari
(The Wetlands & Wildlife Natural
Reserve of Vendicari)
5 Marzamemi
6 Ispica
7 Modica
8 Scicli
9 Ragusa
10 Chiaramonte Gulfi

Where to Stay & Dine

Casa Talia **11**
Hotel Novecento **12**
La Gazza Ladra **13**
Majore **14**
Pomodoro **15**

--- Ferry Route

Southeastern Sicily is endowed with treasures—Siracusa was one of the most important cities of the Ancient World. Here is a milky way of UNESCO Sites—all rebuilt after the earthquake of 1693. Just as they have risen from the ashes, so too have the old traditions, now embraced by brigades of young chefs and hoteliers who revel in the riches of this fertile region.

❶ Siracusa. The archeological site of Siracusa was founded as a Greek colony in 733 BC, reputedly prompted by Greece's Oracle of Delphi and attracted by the area's natural harbors, fertile land, fresh springs, and easily defended island, Ortygia. *For more information, see Chapters 3 (p 59) and 6 (p 136).*

From Siracusa, drive west on the SP14, and then the SS287 and SS124 to Palazzolo Acreide. Distance: 41km (25½ miles).

❷ Palazzolo Acreide. Founded in 664, this Baroque town was originally a Greek colony belonging to Siracusa, and is now a UNESCO site. While you're here, stroll around the neighboring **Archeological Park Akrei** (☎ 0931-881499; daily 9am–7pm; €2), to see the ruins of the temples to Persephone and Aphrodite, and the 600-seat **Teatro Greco**, which is still used for performances in summer. A short walk outside the old city brings you to the **Santoni** (Big Saints)—huge statues of fertility goddess Cybele and her ilk that are hewn into the rock. *For more information, see Chapter 3, p 61.*

From Palazzolo Acreide, drive southeast on the SS124, and then continue on the SS287 following the signs to Noto. Distance: 30km (18¾ miles).

❸ Noto. Nicknamed *Il Giardino di Pietra* (Garden of Stone), this UNESCO site represents the pinnacle of Sicilian Baroque. Treat yourself to a stroll around this gorgeous town with a *gelato* (ice cream) from

Siracusa archaeological area.

Cala Mosche, part of the Natural Reserve of Vendicari.

Costanzo (Via Spaventa, 7, near Palazzo Duceziio; ☎ **0931-835243**). This is one of Sicily's most famous *gelaterie*—try the unusual jasmine and rose flavor, redolent of the island's Arabic heritage. *For more information, see Chapters 3 (p 59) and 6 (p 118).*

From Noto, follow the signs for Siracusa and then the SS115 Siracusa/Pachino. Take the SP19 signposted to Portalpo and look for the sign to the Cala Mosche beach. Distance: 13¾km (8½ miles).

❹ Riserva Naturale Oasi Faunistica di Vendicari (The Wetlands & Wildlife Natural Reserve of Vendicari). This is an enchanting stretch of wild coastal nature reserve, composed of white sand beaches and salt lakes that attract 200 species of migratory birds as well as the indigenous water birds. There are several observation hides and well-marked paths fringed with bamboo forest that lead down to the coast, the highlight of which is Cala

Mosche—a crescent-shaped soft sandy beach framed by cliffs. This is among Sicily's most beautiful bays and plans are afoot to encourage turtles to return to what was once their favorite nesting area. 🕐 *2hrs. Main entrance Pantano Grande.* ☎ *0931-571457. Daily summer 7am–8pm & till 6:30pm in winter; free but small parking fee.*

From Riserva di Vendicari, continue on the SP19 south and then left onto the SP85 for Marzamemi. Distance: 14½km (9 miles).

❺ Marzamemi. This attractive fishing village was once important for tuna, as you will see from the former *tonnara* (tuna factory) and warehouses that are now a series of bars and restaurants. Very popular in high summer with tourists and yachties from the burgeoning marina, it's nonetheless still a working fishing village where lobster pots and fishing nets dry in the sun alongside basking cats. A former feudal domain, there's a crumbling noble *palazzo* and a lichen-covered church built of local mellow limestone. To enjoy the bounty of the sea in the picturesque former *tonnara*, try the restaurant **La Cialoma** (Piazza Regina Margherita; ☎ **0931-841772**; menus around €25). Named after the song traditionally sung to round up fishermen at the start of the *mattanza* (tuna slaughter, see p 47), this restaurant is owned by the niece of the last *rais*—the head tuna fisherman. ⏱ *2–3 hrs.*

From Marzamemi, take the SP85, and then the SP22 that becomes the SP49, following the signs to Ispica. Distance: 25km (15½ miles).

⑥ Ispica. This hilltown has a pleasant enough Baroque heart, but its chief claim to fame is the nearby troglodyte city that was inhabited from Neolithic times to the early 20th century. The **Cava d'Ispica** (daily summer 9am–7pm, Nov–Mar Mon–Sat 9am–1:15pm) is an 11km (7-mile) limestone gorge, honeycombed with cave dwellings, rock

art, and prehistoric tombs. Luckily, the best are close to the entrance to the site at the northern end of the gorge. The southern part of the gorge nearest to Ispica town is the **Parco Archaeologico della Forza** (daily 9am–1 hr before sunset), where a well-marked path leads past ancient cave dwellings and church ruins up to a viewing point with the gorge spread out in front of you. In the town itself, walk down from the castle past the house where Nobel prize-winning poet Salvatore Quasimodo was born and you come to a remarkable little row of houses. Standing half in and half out of the rock, they are known to the locals as *grotte vestite* (dressed caves). ⏱ *2 hrs.*

From Ispica, take the SS115 signposted to Módica, and then right onto the SP43. Distance: 17½km (10¾ miles).

⑦ Modica. Modica is another Baroque jewel set in the eroded,

Marzamemi marina.

rugged landscape of the **Monti Iblei** along with **Ragusa** and **Scicli**. It lost out to Ragusa in its bid to become the capital of the newly created province in 1927, but today is a thriving Baroque town with a new prosperity in the air. Milanese architects are buying up old town houses, restaurants are going upmarket, and boutique hotels are opening. *For more information on Modica, see Chapter 3. Tourist information: Via Grimaldi, 32.* ☎ *0932-762626. Mon–Sat 8:30am–1:30pm and 3–7pm. Sun 8:30am–1:30pm.*

From Modica, follow the signs to Scicli going south on the SP54. Distance: 10½km (6½ miles).

⑧ Scicli. Lying on the same latitude as Tunis, this is like a small-scale Modica and is the only town of any size between Ragusa and the sea. Life is slow and typically Sicilian in this attractive Baroque town with its ochre-colored façades. In recent years it has had a fair amount of restoration and now it even has its first boutique hotel, the Hotel Novecento (see 'Where to Stay & Dine', p 99). The main square, **Piazza Italia**, is graced by *palazzi* with fantastically adorned balconies and 18th-century churches such as the Baroque

Cathedral, **Sant'Ignazio**. Nearby, just to the north, is the elegant church of **San Giovanni** whose exuberant exterior is matched by an interior that's equally impressive. Also, don't miss the beautiful balconies of the **Palazzo Beneventano** (Via Tripoli, closed to the public), adorned with fantastical mythical beasts, grotesque cherubs, and manic, ghoulish human faces. A path leads from here up to a ruined castle and a terrific viewpoint by the abandoned 11th-century church **Chiesa San Matteo**. It's said that secret passageways, used during the Saracen sieges, lead from here out of town, and the hill is honeycombed with some that were inhabited as recently as the 1980s. Every May the festival of *Madonna delle Milizie* re-enacts a battle between the Saracens and Normans—won with the help of the Madonna by the Normans. *For more information, see Chapter 3, p 60.*

From Scicli, take the SP54 and then the SS115 to Ragusa. Distance: 25½km (16 miles).

⑨ Ragusa. Your first sight of Ragusa Ibla is likely to be a honey-colored revelation. A tumble of domes, towers, *palazzi*, and houses

View over Ragusa's honey colored buildings.

cling to a rocky spur like a gorgeous film set. This is a town with two identities: **Ragusa Superiore** (Upper Town) is the 'new' town constructed in a grid pattern after the 1693 earthquake, while **Ragusa Ibla** is a maze of medieval streets, many of which are mercifully traffic-free. *For more information, see Chapters 3 (p 29 and p 61) and 6 (p 133).*

From Ragusa, follow the signs to Catania/Agrigento, and then the SP10 and SP8 signposted to Chiaramonte Gulfi. Distance: 18½km (11½ miles).

🔟 **Chiaramonte Gulfi.** This pleasing Baroque town, built in silvery-gray limestone, lives up to its reputation as a 'balcony of Sicily', thanks to its glorious countryside views from the belvedere at the top of the town. Although severely damaged by the 1693 earthquake, the medieval center (*centro storico*) with its cobbled streets, churches,

and *palazzi* has been preserved. The **Arco dell'Annunziata** is the one remaining gateway entrance to the town of the original three. Look too for the cathedral of **Santa Maria Nova** whose Baroque façade is currently being renovated. The town is famous for salamis and cured hams as well as for its high-quality olive oil. There is a charming little olive oil museum, **Museo dell'Olio** with old olive presses and implements used in the process of extracting the oil from the olives. There are also seven other small museums, the most interesting of which is one devoted to musical instruments and another, the **Casa Museo Liberty**, dedicated to the Italian Art Nouveau style. Entrance to each museum is €1 (€4 for all eight). *Museo dell'Olio, Palazzo Montesano, Via Montesano.* ☎ *0932-711239. Admission €1. Wed–Sat 9am–1pm and Fri 4–7pm, Sat 3:30–7:30pm, Sun 9:30am–12:30pm and 3:30–7:30pm.*

Where to **Stay & Dine**

★★ **Casa Talia** MODICA   A neo-boho style B&B, designed by its Milanese architect owners, stunningly set on a clifftop. There are six rooms and two terrace gardens shaded by gnarled olive trees and lemon trees. The views across the valley to the Cathedral of San Giorgio are as unforgettable as this delectable designer establishment. *Via Exaudinos 1/9.* ☎ *0932-752075. www. casatalia.it. 6 units. Doubles €130–150. MC, V.*

★★ **Hotel Novecento** SCICLI   This seven room townhouse is Scicli's first boutique hotel (opened in 2008). Set in the heart of the Baroque *centro storico*, the Baroque theme is continued inside with

exposed honey-stone arches, neo-Baroque sofas and armchairs, and frescoed ceilings all blended with cutting-edge design bathrooms and fittings. Very friendly, attentive service. *Via Dupré, 11.* ☎ *0932-843817. www.hotel900.it. Doubles €110–150. AE, MC, V.*

★★★ **La Gazza Ladra** MODICA   This Michelin-starred restaurant is overseen by chef Accursio Craparo who skillfully interprets local traditional dishes with inventive zeal. Signature dishes include *spaghetti con spremuta siciliana*— a delicious savory mix of local oranges, anchovies, cinnamon, wild fennel olives, pistachios, and almonds with the most succulent pasta. To follow, try the *sorbetto di pistacchio e basilica con grano cotto* (basil and pistachio sorbet with *grano* cheese). The décor is soberly elegant, the service impeccable, and for such a gourmet, Michelin-starred experience, your pockets don't need to be too deep. *The restaurant belongs to the 19th-century historic hotel Palazzo Failla. Via Blandini, 5.* ☎ *0932-941059. www.palazzofailla. it. It has 10 antique bedrooms, some with stunning ceiling frescoes. Doubles €125–175. La Gazza Ladra, Via Blandini, 11.* ☎ *0932-755655. www. ristorantelagazzaladra.it. Menus €45–67 AE, MC, V. Closed Sun eve & Mon.*

★ **Majore** CHIARAMONTE GULFI The motto of this restaurant—*Qui si magnifica il porco* (here pork is glorified)—is shown in a fresco in the rustic dining room. Established since 1986, the current Lattera-Majores owners are the fourth generation specializing in the versatility of this animal. Home-made salamis, stuffed ribs, *capicollo* (coarse pork

sausage) and *falsomagro* (stuffed pork rolls) all feature, but there are also delicious cheeses and spectacular Sicilian desserts on offer. There is an excellent wine cellar that you can visit. The restaurant also has a butcher's shop where you can buy to take away. *Via Martiri Ungheresi, 12.* ☎ *0932-928019. www.majore.it. Menus €14–21. AE, MC, V. Open lunch and dinner Tues–Sun. Closed July.*

★ **Pomodoro** SCICLI Scicli has a little way to go before it earns too many foodie plaudits, but it's getting there and this modern, reasonably priced restaurant is a great find, with its friendly and informal service. Start with the delicious homemade bread and dip liberally into the local extra virgin olive oils, followed perhaps with tartlets of melted *Ragusano* cheese, honey, balsamic vinegar, and cabbage. *Corso Garibaldi, 46.* ☎ *0932-931444. Menus €24–40. No credit cards. Open Wed–Mon lunch and dinner.* ●

Caltagirone

Viale Regina Elena

S. Giorgio

Via Gerbino

Via L. Sturzo

Via S. Salvatore

10

Via S. Sofia

Via Cappuccini

Via Circonvallazione di Levante

7

6 **11**

8 **9** **Municipio**

S. Giacomo

Via Celso

Piazza Municipio

Gesù

Piazza Marcinno

Via Cristoforo Colombo

Via Madonna d. Stella

5 *Piazza Umberto I.*

4

Via Circonvallazione

Ponte San Francesco

Via Acquanuova Seconda

3

S. Pietro

Via Roma

Via G. Arcoleo

S. Francesco di Paola

1

2

Viale Principe Maria Jose

Via S. Maria di Gesù

† Church

☒ Post Office

ⓘ Information

1 Museo della Cerámica
2 Giardino della Villa
3 San Francesco d'Assisi all'Immacolata
4 Museo Civico
5 Cattedrale di San Giuliano
6 Scala di Santa Maria del Monte
7 Santa Maria del Monte
8 Giardino Spadaro

Where to Stay & Dine

Il Palazzo dei Marchesi di Santa Barbara **9**
La Piazzetta **10**
La Scala **11**
NH Villa San Mauro **12**
Villa Tasca **13**

12

13

This golden sandstone city is a UNESCO World Heritage Site, set between the Iblei and Erei hills. Its name derives from the Arabic Qal'at Ghiran, loosely translated as 'Castle of Vases'. For centuries, Caltagirone had a flourishing ceramics industry, but under Arab domination techniques were passed on, such as the blue and yellow glazing and typically intricate designs. START: **Caltagirone is 30km (19 miles) southeast of Piazza Armerina and about 40 minutes by road from Catania.**

❶ ★ Museo della Cerámica. Clay deposits and abundant wood from the surrounding forests provide the tools for the local pottery industry. The museum has a good collection of Bronze Age pots and Greek and Roman artifacts. In the Middle Ages section, Arab vases, trademark Sicilian ware, and storage jars for the local medieval honey industry make an appearance. Also on display are a collection of more recent pharmacy jars and glazed vases. 🕐 *30 min. Viale Giardini Pubblici/Via Roma.* ☎ *0933-58418. Admission €3. Daily 9am–6:30pm.*

❷ Giardino della Villa. Beside the Museo della Cerámica, these gardens make a pleasant, shady

spot for a picnic. Originally designed by Giovanni Battista Basile in the mid-1800s, they contain many colorful touches such as the Moorish, Art Nouveau bandstand, which is festooned with ceramic tiles. 🕐 *½ hr. Viale Giardini Pubblici/Via Roma. Open all times.*

❸ San Francesco d'Assisi all'Immacolata. You can't miss the spire of this Sicilian Baroque church. Founded in the 12th century, it was razed by the 1693 earthquake then rebuilt in Baroque style with a splendid 18th-century façade. Take a look too at the Ponte San Francesco that leads to the church and which is decorated with tiles. 🕐 *20 min. Piazza San Francesco.*

Ceramic mural, Caltagirone.

Mon–Sat 8am–8pm, but times variable.

4 Museo Cívico. Set in a former 17th-century Bourbon prison, this museum contains a variety of archeological finds from the 6th century BC to the present. The museum's art gallery shows the town's rich artistic heritage before and after the earthquake, including paintings by the Vaccaro family who renovated the Cathedral. ⏱ *30 min. Via Roma, 10.* ☎ *0933-31590. Free admission. Tues–Sat 9:30am–1:30pm, Sun 9:30am–12:30pm, and Tues–Sun 4–5pm.*

Tip

The town has two Tourist Information Centers, the first at *Galleria Luigi Sturzo, Piazza Municipio.* ☎ *0933-41365. www.comune.caltagirone.ct.it. Mon–Sat 9am–7pm, Sun 9am–1pm and 3–7pm.* The main tourist office is in the upper town in Via Volta Libertini (just off Piazza Umberto). ☎ *0933-53809. Mon–Fri 8am–2:30pm and 3–6pm.*

Scala di Santa Maria del Monte.

5 Cattedrale di San Giuliano. Dominating **Piazza Umberto I**, the cathedral's origins date to Norman times. It subsequently had a Baroque makeover, but now has many 20th-century features, including the façade and the *campanile* (belltower). Inside there's a beautiful 16th-century wooden crucifix. ⏱ *20 min. Piazza Umberto I.*

6 ★★★ Scala di Santa Maria del Monte. This spectacular set of 142 ceramic steps, built in the 1600s, is the landmark of the city. They lead from Piazza Municipio up the hill to the church of Santa Maria del Monte. Each step is decorated with different hand-crafted ceramics, installed in the 1950s by local ceramicists. Some portray mythical and heraldic themes, others are purely abstract, and some are decorative, geometric patterns. No two are alike. They certainly add color to a fairly strenuous climb. In the last two weeks of May, Caltagirone stages the '**Infiorita**' festival when the steps are covered in a huge floral display. And, on the 24–25th July, they are lit with thousands of colored paper lanterns in the **Illuminata** festival, to honor the town's patron saint, San Giacomo. The staircase is lined with tempting ceramic galleries and workshops. The town is also famous for *presepi* (nativity crib figurines) made of both terracotta and ceramics. ⏱ *45 min.*

7 Santa Maria del Monte. Santa Maria del Monte, the former Cathedral of Caltagirone, crowns the steps of La Scala. Constructed in the mid-16th century, and rebuilt after the 1693 earthquake, it's now rather neglected. Nonetheless, the magical views over the town from its slender belltower are worth the climb. ⏱ *15 min. Top of Scala di Santa Maria del Monte. Opening hours variable, normally 8am–noon, 4–7pm.*

♨ ★ Giardino Spadaro. Chill out in this shady garden bar close to La Scala, serving snacks such as panini and long, cool drinks. It gets very busy in the evenings. *Via San Giuseppe. Open all day Wed–Mon. $.*

Tip

Parking is available in a public car park near Chiesa San Francesco di Paola, just before you reach Piazza Umberto. You can buy parking tickets at various bars and tobacco shops throughout town.

Where to **Stay**

★★ NH Villa San Mauro NEW TOWN   Near the hospital, this elegant four star-hotel is well-run and pleasantly decorated with plenty of Caltagirone ceramics, a swimming pool, and a good restaurant that specializes in traditional Sicilian dishes. Parking is available. *Via Portosalvo, 14.* ☎ *0933-26500. www. nh-hotels.it. 91 units. Doubles €110–165. AE, MC, V.*

★ Villa Tasca STRADA STATALE (5km/3 miles north)   This elegant country manor house, in a gloriously unspoiled locale, is a great example of *turismo rurale* (rural tourism). The 10 rooms are pleasingly furnished in traditional Sicilian style. There's an outdoor swimming pool and horse riding is also on offer. Book in advance to enjoy the restaurant's local, seasonal specialties. *Contrada Fontana Pietra S.P. 37/11.* ☎ *0933-22760. www.villatasca.it. Doubles €90–150. MC, V. Closed 10th Jan–10th Feb and 5th–30th Nov.*

Where to **Dine**

★★ Il Palazzo dei Marchesi di Santa Barbara CENTRO STORICO Dine under frescoed ceilings in the grandest restaurant in town, fittingly set in an 18th-century *palazzo*. The service is attentive and the well-crafted Sicilian cooking superb, but the full-on lighting may not be to everyone's taste. *Via San Bonaventura, 22.* ☎ *0933-22406. Menus €25–40. Closed Mon.*

★ La Piazzetta CENTRO STORICO Expect home-made pasta dishes and regional Sicilian specialties at this popular little restaurant. *Via Vespri, 20.* ☎ *0933-24178. Menus*

from €20. MC, V. Open Fri–Wed; closed mid-Aug–mid-Sep.

★ La Scala HISTORIC CENTER   Set in an 18th-century palazzo, this restaurant at the foot of the famous steps in the heart of town has a massive following. In summer you can dine alfresco in the courtyard where a mountain stream is visible through glass panels, running beneath the floor. The local Sicilian fare is complemented by good, local wines. *Scalinata Santa Maria del Monte 8.* ☎ *0933-57781. Menus €25–35. MC, V. Open Thurs–Tues lunch and dinner.*

Catania

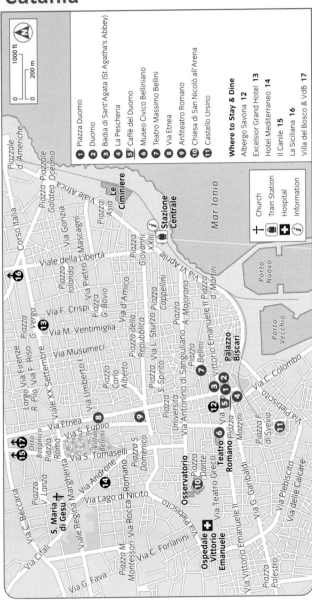

1 Piazza Duomo
2 Duomo
3 Badia di Sant'Agata (St Agatha's Abbey)
4 La Pescheria
5 Caffè del Duomo
6 Museo Civico Belliniano
7 Teatro Massimo Bellini
8 Via Etnea
9 Anfiteatro Romano
10 Chiesa di San Nicolò all'Arena
11 Castello Ursino

Where to Stay & Dine

Albergo Savona 12
Excelsior Grand Hotel 13
Hotel Mediterraneo 14
Il Canile 15
La Siciliana 16
Villa del Bosco & VdB 17

+ Church
▪ Train Station
✚ Hospital
ⓘ Information

Sicily's second largest city is known as the 'city of black and white', after the lava and white marble of its architecture. Wiped off the map at least seven times by earthquakes and the wrath of Mt. Etna, it always bounces back. Indeed, its burgeoning economy, wide boulevards, grandiose architecture, and vibrant atmosphere have earned it the nickname: 'Milano of the South'.

1 ★ Piazza Duomo. Created by the city's planner, Vaccarini (1702–68), this Baroque square is the heart of Catania, and is dominated by the **Duomo** (Cathedral). The **Fontana dell'Elefante** (Elephant Fountain, 1735) is a symbol of the city, carved from Mt. Etna's black lava with a comical, smiley face.

2 ★ Duomo. Catania's Cathedral with its splendid Baroque façade actually dates from Norman times, but it was destroyed in the earthquake of 1693. During reconstruction, its granite columns were 'borrowed' from the city's Roman amphitheater. Inside on the right-hand side you come to the composer Vincenzo Bellini's tomb,

guarded by a life-size marble angel. 🕑 *30 min. Piazza Duomo.* ☎ *095-320044. Free admission. Daily 7am–noon and 4:30–7pm. Museo: Via Etnea 8.* ☎ *095-281635. Admission €4.30 adults, €2.50 children under 18. Tues–Sun 9am–2:30pm and 4–7:30pm.*

3 Badia di Sant'Agata (St Agata's Abbey). This church beside the Duomo is another Vaccarini masterpiece. Built in 1735–67, the octagonal interior is a splendid example of Rococo decoration, although this was completed after Vaccarini's death. 🕑 *15 min. Via Vittorio Emanuele II. Free admission. Mon–Sat 7:30–noon. Sun 4–7:30.*

Piazza Duomo, Catania.

St Agatha's Abbey.

5 **Caffè del Duomo.** This is the most charming café on the main piazza, with its Belle Epoque style, marble counters, a lavish tavola calda (hot table) offering all kinds of tasty snacks, and vibrantly-colored fruits made of marzipan. *Piazza Duomo 12.* ☎ *095-7150556. Daily from 5:30am–midnight.*

6 **Museo Civico Belliniano.** A rather drab apartment was the birthplace of Catania's famous son, the composer Vincenzo Bellini (1801–34). Here you can see original folios of his operas (such as *La Straniera, Sonnambula, Norma, I Puritani,* and *I Cavalieri*) alongside his harpsichords, pianos, and death mask. The guest book is a roll call of the world's most famous musicians, including signatures from Pavarotti and Carlo Muti. ⏱ *45 min. Piazza San Francesco 3.* ☎ *095-7150535. Free admission. Mon–Sat 9am–1pm and Tues and Thurs 3–6pm.*

4 ★★★ **La Pescheria.** The warren of streets behind the **Piazza del Duomo** come to life each morning for the island's most colorful fish market—La Pescheria—with every size and type of fish laid out amid a cacophony of shouting and activity. 'If it swims we Catanians eat it,' say the local fishmongers. ⏱ *30 min. Mon–Sat dawn till late morning.*

7 ★★★ **Teatro Massimo Bellini.** Inspired by the Empire-style Opéra Garnier in Paris, this is among Europe's grandest opera houses. In the foyer is a splendid statue of Bellini himself. Inside, the acoustics would make the great

La Pescheria.

Taking the Air

At the far end of Via Etnea, the green public gardens of Villa Bellini are a welcome oasis away from the city heat and congestion. Among the exotic plants is a huge fig tree—claimed by the Catanians to be the world's largest. The jury may be out on this but what is certain is that this is one of Sicily's most attractive public parks. It spreads over several hills, from where there are excellent vistas of Mt. Etna.

composer proud. Some of Italy's best operas and concerts are staged here and nothing could be more fitting than hearing Bellini's *Norma* on his home turf. It was this opera that was presented on the day of the theater's inauguration on 31st May, 1890. *Piazza Teatro Massimo, Via Perrotta Giuseppe, 12, facing Piazza Bellini.* ☎ *095-7306111. www.teatromassimobellini.it. Box office open Mon–Sat 9:30am–12:30pm and Tues–Fri 5–7pm.*

8 Via Etnea. The city's main artery is a wide boulevard running north from **Piazza del Duomo** up to the flanks of **Mt. Etna**. It's full of shops and cafés and you'll find plenty of outdoor terraces to enjoy a drink or snack. Try the traditional Catanian thirst-quencher—soda water with crushed lemon (with or without salt).

9 Anfiteatro Romano. Built on the site of an earlier Greek Theater, the present remains of the Roman Theater, built from lava blocks, are estimated to date from the 2nd century AD. The ruins lie below street level, but the gladiator tunnels are still visible where wild beasts shipped from Africa paced before doing grisly battle with the gladiators. Only a small part has been excavated, but it was once one of the largest of all Roman amphitheaters, believed to have held up to

17,000 spectators. Close your eyes and let your imagination run wild in this atmospheric spot. ⊕ *30 min. Piazza Stesicoro, Via Vittorio Emanuele, 266 (half way up Via Etnea).* ☎ *095-7150405. Free admission. Daily 9am–1:30pm and 3–7pm.*

10 Chiesa di San Nicolò all'Arena. Built on the site of a Benedictine monastery, this is Sicily's largest and possibly its spookiest church. The façade is brutalist at worst, ugly at best, with pillars sticking up like tusks. The interior is cavernous and rather bare, except for the sculpted choir stalls. In 1841, a meridian line was laid in the transept floor to catch the sunlight at noon. Nowadays, due to the movement of the volcanic land, it catches the sun at 12:13pm. The church was reconstructed after the 1693 earthquake, but despite sporadic renovations, it remains unfinished. ⊕ *20 min. Piazza Dante.* ☎ *095-312366. Free admission. Daily 9am–1pm and also Tues and Thurs 3–6pm.*

11 Castello Ursino. This fortress, belonging to Frederick ll in the 13th century, is one of the few remains of medieval Catania. It was originally sited on a promontory overlooking the Ionian sea, but Mt. Etna's activity has shifted the land over the centuries and the castle is now landlocked. Walking along the perimeter you can still see the old moats and

Castello Ursino, Catania.

some Renaissance windows in the south side. The **Museo Civico** looks down into the foundations and displays mosaic fragments, inscriptions, and tombstones. There's a permanent art gallery too of mainly Sicilian or South Italian works dating to the 1400s. ⏱ *45 min. Piazza Federici du Svevia. ☎ 095-345830. Free admission. Mon–Sat 9am–1pm and 3–7pm. Temporary exhibitions on the ground floor.*

Where to **Stay**

★ **Albergo Savona** HISTORIC CENTER Just a two minute walk from the Duomo, this family-run hotel has three floors of quiet rooms accessed via a grand flight of marble-capped stairs. Some rooms have views of the Duomo. *Via Vittorio Emanuele 210. ☎ 095-326982. www.hotelsavona.it. 30 units. Doubles €70–140. AE, DC, MC, V.*

★★ **Excelsior Grand Hotel** NORTH OF PIAZZA DEL DUOMO Catania's most prestigious hotel, built in 1954, boasts plush deluxe rooms, opulent marble bathrooms, a top-notch restaurant, and a stately façade. Ask for a room with a balcony overlooking the lovely Piazza Verga and Mt. Etna beyond. *Piazza Verga, 39. ☎ 095-7476111. www.thi.it. 163 units. Doubles €220–260. AE, DC, MC, V.*

★ **Hotel Mediterraneo** HISTORIC CENTER This three star hotel is one of Catania's most modern, set in a residential area but only a stone's throw from the center. Rooms are simple and unfussy with large windows, and bathrooms have both tub and shower. *Via Dottor Consoli 27. ☎ 095-325330. www. hotelmditerraneoct.com. 63 units. Doubles €115–165. AE, MC, V.*

★★★ Villa del Bosco & VdB

NORTH OF VIA ETNEA   Built originally in 1826 as a palatial home, this villa is now an elegant boutique hotel festooned with antiques and marble (see also 'Il Canile' restaurant below). *Via del Bosco 62.* ☎ *095-7335100. www.hotelvillavdbnext.it. 52 units. Doubles €165–240. AE, DC, MC, V.*

Where to **Dine**

★★ Il Canile NORTH OF VIA ETNEA

The name of this elegant frescoed restaurant (located in the Villa del Bosco hotel, see above) translates as 'The Kennel'—taken from the pair of 18th-century stone dogs that stand guard near the entrance. Fine, regional specialties feature, including locally gathered *porcini* mushrooms from the flanks of Mt. Etna (in season). *Villa del Bosco, Via del Bosco 62.* ☎ *095-7335100. Reservations recommended. Menus €30–35. AE, MC, V. Lunch and dinner daily.*

★ La Siciliana NORTH OF CENTER

Founded in 1968 and still in the hands of the original family, this stylish restaurant is set in a 19th-century villa. The cuisine is traditional with an innovative twist and an emphasis on fish dishes. In summer you can dine alfresco on the garden terrace. *Viale Marco Polo 52A.* ☎ *095-376400. www.lasiciliana.it. Reservations required. Menus €31–42. AE, DC, MC, V. Lunch Tues–Sun; dinner Tues–Sat.*

Nightlife in Catania

The city buzzes after dark and has the liveliest nightlife on the island. At the touristy heart, there are plenty of outdoor cafés on the Piazza del Duomo. The student quarter is around the Piazza Bellini and Via Vasta (off Via Etnea) where there are plenty of late-night bars. **Perbacco! Wine Bar** on the Via Vasta (☎ **347-0937988**) is full of squishy sofas where the Catanians come to sip wine till the early hours. Near the Stazione Centrale (railway station), **Zo** (Piazzale Asia, 6; ☎ **095-533871**), is the talk of the town—a former sulfur works now converted to a cutting edge contemporary arts center with great food, sounds, and experimental art. For aficionados of Cuba and Che Guevara, the **Nievski Pub** (Via Alessi 15–17; ☎ **095-313792**) is a great alternative bar/trattoria—with good beer, too.

Cefalù

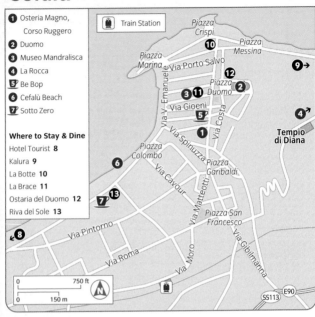

1. Osteria Magno,
   Corso Ruggero
2. Duomo
3. Museo Mandralisca
4. La Rocca
5. Be Bop
6. Cefalù Beach
7. Sotto Zero

Where to Stay & Dine

Hotel Tourist 8
Kalura 9
La Botte 10
La Brace 11
Ostaria del Duomo 12
Riva del Sole 13

Train Station

Piazza Crispi
Piazza Messina
Piazza Marina
Via Porto Salvo
Piazza Duomo
Via V. Emanuele
Via Gioeni
Via Costa
Tempio di Diana
Via Spinuzza
Piazza Colombo
Piazza Garibaldi
Via Cavour
Via Matteotti
Piazza San Francesco
Via Gibilmanna
Via Pintorno
Via Moro
Via Roma
SS113
E90

0   750 ft
0   150 m

Caught between a rocky crag and a crescent-shaped bay is picturesque Cefalù. Its origins date at least to Greek times—the name derives from the Ancient Greek word for 'cape'—but the present-day town, with its *tagliatelle* of medieval streets, was built largely at the behest of a Norman King, Roger II. The town is also a good starting point for treks in the Madonie mountains to the south. START: 81km (50 miles) E of Palermo, 170km (106 miles) W of Messina.

1 Osteria Magno, Corso Ruggero. Away from the medieval center, the Corso Ruggero is the main street in town, starting at **Piazza Garibaldi,** one of the four gateways to Cefalù. It's a pedestrian street, and so perfect for strolling, shopping, and looking at the façades of the various *palazzi* in this area. *Palazzo* Osteria Magno (corner of Via Amendola and Corso Ruggero) is of particular interest. It was originally the home of Roger II, but extensively altered and renovated over

the years, and is now a venue for temporary art exhibitions. Drop into the tourist office across the road for details of what's on. 🕐 *40 min. Corso Ruggero, 116.* ☎ *0921-421050. www.cefalu-tour.pa.it.*

2 ★★★ Duomo. This splendid example of 'Sicilian Romanesque' is twinned with the Duomo in Monreale and the Palatine Church in Palermo—all of which are star sights. Legend says that when Roger II was lost at sea and about to perish in a violent storm, in desperation he prayed to God that if his life were spared he would build a fine cathedral in the Almighty's honor. His wish was granted and in 1131 the order was given for construction of the Duomo. The city's shield bears the theme of miracles and gratitude, depicted by loaves and fishes. With its twin towers and mighty façade visible from miles around, it seems more fortress than cathedral. But the jewels are within—in the apse and vault, where you will be dazzled by the oldest Byzantine-Norman mosaics in Sicily, dating from 1150–1160. 🕐 45 min. *Piazza del Duomo.* ☎ *0921-922021. Free admission but donations welcomed. Daily 8am–noon, 3:30–7pm. but closed during church services.*

Tip

Try to get to the Duomo early to avoid the coach parties. Alternatively, arrive in the late afternoon when the façade appears to shimmer, bathed in golden light.

❸ ★★ **Museo Mandralisca.** A steepish walk from the Duomo leads down to this museum with its rather dusty collection of ancient artifacts, coins, medals, Madonnas, and bucket-loads of shells. Its highlight, however, is the ★★ *Portrait of an Unknown Man* (c. 1460) by Antonello da Messina (1430–79), Sicily's most eminent artist. This painting is his earliest known work. Baron Enrico di Mandralisca, who lived here in the 19th century and founded the collection, bought the painting from a pharmacy on the Aeolian island of Lipari, where it had been used as a cabinet door. Apparently an assistant working there scratched the unknown man's face to pay him back for his sneering expression. 🕐 40 min. *Via Mandralisca 13.* ☎ *0921-421547. www. museomandralisca.it. Admission €6. Daily 9am–7pm.*

❹ ★★★ **La Rocca.** This great, craggy mass looms over the town. An ascent is quite a challenge—especially in the summer heat—but your efforts will be rewarded with

Cefalù's Duomo houses the oldest Byzantine-Norman mosaics in Sicily.

View of Cefalù and La Rocca from the sea.

some of Sicily's most dazzling views. From Piazza Garibaldi a sign indicates the start of the climb: the lower part is cobbled with handrails, although quite steep. Farther up the path becomes quite rough and it's a good 20 minute climb up to the ruins of the 5th-century BC **Tempio di Diana** (Temple of Diana). Count on another 45 minutes to reach the ancient Arab and medieval fortifications at the top and spectacular

views from Capo d'Orlando in the east to Palermo in the west. 🕐 *3 hrs.*

5 **Be Bop.** Set around an attractive courtyard, this all-day pub serves tasty hot and cold food. There's live music at the weekends when it buzzes until 4am. *Via Nicola Botta, 4.* ☎ *0921-923972. $.*

Tip

The best time to do this climb in summer is early morning or when evening breezes will cool you down. But at whatever time of the day, you'll need strong walking shoes, a bottle of water, sun protection, and plenty of puff.

6 ★★ kids **Cefalù Beach.** Cefalù's long, sandy, crescent-shaped beach is possibly the best along the northern coast. However, it does get very crowded in high season. There's free beach access at the eastern end of the sandy beach—but it's probably worth

The busy beach at Cefalù.

Parco Naturale Regionale delle Madonie

From Cefalù, it's 13½km (8½ miles) south to the village of Gibilmanna, with magnificent views across the **Parco Naturale Regionale delle Madonie**. This huge park covers 39,679 hectares (98,049 acres) and has many hiking routes that vary in length and difficulty. Around Gibilmanna especially, there are plenty of superb trails, some combining walking with visits to towns and villages. Serious hikers can climb **Pizzo Carbonara** (1,979m/6,492ft), Sicily's highest peak after Mt. Etna. Maps and useful information on the area are available from the **Tourist Office** (Via Umberto; ☎ 0921-671124; www. comune.castelbuono.pa.it). A route of 17½km (11 miles) southeast leads to the attractive mountain town of **Castelbuono**, the 'capital' of the Madonie. Castelbuono's **Museo di Mina Palumbo** (Via Roma, 52; ☎ 0921-676596; daily 9am–1pm and 3–7pm; €6) is named after the late naturalist Palumbo and devoted to the Madonie's natural history and botany. For detailed information of the area, visit www.parcodellemadonie.it and www.madonie.it.

paying for the comfortable sunbeds, umbrellas, and facilities at one of the Lidi, such as Lido Poseidon. *For more information on beaches, see Chapter 4.*

Travel Tip

Getting around Cefalù on foot is easy—no cars are allowed in the historic core. The promenade, Via Lungomare G. Giardino, is lined with cafés and restaurants and is the place to be for the early evening passeggiata.

🔲 **Sotto Zero.** At the beginning of the lungomare (seafront), this Buddha Bar-styled bar is a great place to chill out. *Open all day.*

Where to **Stay**

★ **Hotel Tourist** SEAFRONT, OUT OF TOWN   Don't let the name put you off because this is a good holiday hotel in a tranquil beachside position, about a 15 minute walk along the lungomare. Bedrooms tend to be simply furnished, with shower-only bathrooms, but some have views over the sea with balconies. The hotel also has a private beach. *Lungomare Giardina.* ☎ 0921-421750. www.touristhotel. it. 46 units. €90–200. AE, MC, V.

★ **kids Kalura** EAST, OUT OF TOWN Set on a little promontory 3km (2 miles) east along the coast, this palm-shaded hotel is reminiscent of a North African retreat. It's very family-oriented with plenty of activities available such as mountain biking, canoes, and riding, as well as a large swimming pool. Most rooms have good views and are well-furnished with shower-only bathrooms. There's also a private beach. *Via Vicenzo Cavallaro 13, Contrada Caldura.* ☎ *0921-421354. www. hotel-kalura.com. 73 units. Doubles €90–270. AE, DC, MC, V.*

★★ Riva del Sole SEAFRONT
This is the best hotel in town, set in a modern building and run by the Cimino family since its opening in 1966. Rooms are light and airy each with a private balcony or veranda—with great views over the sea. Service is attentive and welcoming and there's an intimate bar, panoramic terrace, and very graceful garden. *Lungomare G. Giardino, 25.* ☎ *0921-421230. www.rivadelsole.com. 28 units. Doubles €120–140. AE, MC, V. Closed Nov.*

Where to **Dine**

★ La Botte HISTORIC CENTER
This family-run eaterie just off Corso Ruggero specializes in the freshest fish, along with fine antipasti and pasta dishes. Good service and a warm welcome. *Via Veterani, 6.* ☎ *0921-424315. Menus €24–52. AE, MC, V. Tues–Sun lunch and dinner. Closed lunch from 15th July–30th Aug.*

★ La Brace HISTORIC CENTER
This popular restaurant resembles a little French bistro, hidden in a narrow cobbled street near the Duomo. But the specialties are Sicilian with imaginative international touches. Highlights include *spiedini di pesce spada* (marinated swordfish kebabs), very succulent fillet steak, and fine home-made pasta dishes. Reservations recommended. *Via XXV Novembre 10 (off Corso Ruggero).* ☎ *0921-423570. www.*

The terrace at the Hotel Kalura.

Outdoor tables in Piazza Duomo

ristorantelabrace.com. Menus €16–33. AE, DC, MC, V. Open lunch and dinner Wed–Sun; dinner only Tues. Closed 15th Dec–15th Jan.

★★ Ostaria del Duomo HISTORIC CENTER   For its location right in front of the Duomo, you could be forgiven for thinking that this would be the most expensive and sophisticated restaurant in town. In fact the prices are reasonable, especially given the quality of the cuisine and a wonderful wine list. Try smoked fish, a seafood salad, or carpaccio of beef in the vaulted dining room or alfresco on the cobblestones outside. Reservations recommended. *Via Seminario, 5.* ☎ *0921-421838. www.ostariadelduomo.com. Menus €25–36. AE, DC, MC, V. Tues–Sun noon–midnight. Closed mid-Nov–end Feb.*

Beauty & the Beast

Utterly photogenic, it is no wonder that Cefalù had a starring role in Giuseppe Tornatore's classic romantic film, *Cinema Paradiso* (1989) which won an Oscar. But it was also once the site of the English occultist, Aleister Crowley, who self-styled himself as 'the beast'. In 1920 Crowley founded l´Abbazia di Thelema (the abbey of Thelema) in Cefalù to practise his diabolical 'rights' with a small band of followers. Satanic rituals and orgies held in the villa were the scandalised talk of the area. The community was finally disbanded by Mussolini, condemned by him as a hotbed of free love, bizarre religious practices and drugs and the notorious Crowley was ordered out of Italy. Today the (private) villa is crumbling and unkempt, overshadowed by a modern sports stadium. But Crowley's notoriety lives on. When asked to draw up a list of names to appear on the Beatles' Sgt Pepper album John Lennon included Aleister Crowley, so introducing 'the Beast' to a whole new generation.

Noto

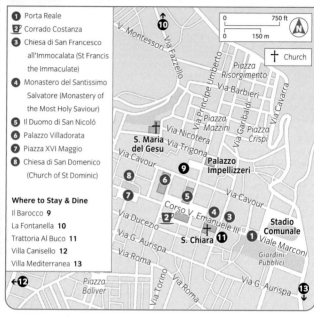

1. Porta Reale
2. Corrado Costanza
3. Chiesa di San Francesco all'Immocalata (St Francis the Immaculate)
4. Monastero del Santissimo Salvatore (Monastery of the Most Holy Saviour)
5. Il Duomo di San Nicoló
6. Palazzo Villadorata
7. Piazza XVI Maggio
8. Chiesa di San Domenico (Church of St Dominic)

Where to Stay & Dine
Il Barocco 9
La Fontanella 10
Trattoria Al Buco 11
Villa Canisello 12
Villa Mediterranea 13

Known as the 'Garden of Stone', Noto is the most beautiful of Sicily's Baroque towns. Another victim of the 1693 earthquake, it has risen phoenix-like and is now a UNESCO World Heritage Site. Since 2002, the town has been almost completely renovated. The local limestone of the buildings takes on a soft peachy-golden glow and the effect, especially at sunset, is spectacular. **START: Noto is 31km (19 miles) SW of Syracuse and 55km (34 miles) E of Ragusa.**

1 Porta Reale. This '**Royal Gate**' is the monumental entrance to the main street, **Corso Vittorio Emanuele**. Notice the three symbols adorning the gate—a swan, dog, and tower—that are representative of the town's former allegiance to the Bourbon monarchy. From here stroll along the Corso Vittorio Emanuele and admire the golden buildings that flank the 1km (approximately ½-mile) long street. Just by the Porta Reale, the **Giardini Pubblici** are pleasant shady gardens full of bougainvillea and palm trees, where locals come to stroll in the evening. ⏱ *20 min.*

2 Corrado Costanza. Famous throughout the world, Corrado Costanza specializes in glorious gelato (ice cream). Choose, if you can, between the yummy flavors and try, too, its other sweet delights, including divine cassata (see p. 173). *Via Silvio Spaventa, 9.* ☎ *0931-835243. $.*

③ Chiesa di San Francesco all'Immocalata (St Francis the Immaculate). Three main piazzas run off the Corso Vittorio Emanuele, the first of which (as you go west) is **Piazza Immacolata**, dominated by theatrical steps leading up to the **Chiesa di San Francesco all'Immocalata**. Don't be put off by the rather austere façade. Inside there's a notable work of the Madonna and Child (1564) by Antonio Monachello, one of the treasured items rescued from the earthquake. ⏱ *20 min. Piazza Immocalata.* ☎ *0931-57319. Daily 8:30am–noon and 4–7:30pm.*

④ Monastero del Santissimo Salvatore (Monastery of the Most Holy Saviour). To the right of the Church of San Francesco, this ancient monastery building is now a seminary that cannot be visited— only admired from the outside. Apart from the watchtower, which rises up from the 18th-century façade, the most striking features of the monastery are the windows, which are adorned with 'pot-bellied' or 'goose-breast' balconies—a typical feature of Noto buildings. They were designed so as to allow ladies in expansive dresses to watch the world go by from the balconies. *Monastero del Santissimo Salvatore, Piazza Immocalata. Not open to the public.*

⑤ ★★ Il Duomo di San Nicoló. Halfway along the Corso you come to the harmonious **Piazza Municipio**, dominated by the **Duomo**, which is accessed by a broad flight of steps. It was designed by Rosario Gagliardi, who was greatly influenced by Borromini's churches in Rome, and completed in 1776. After the dome collapsed in 1996, due to minor earth tremors, it underwent years of restoration. The scaffolding that blighted the cathedral was finally removed in 2007 to reveal its magnificent restoration, and the dome sparkles anew. Some of the cathedral's treasures and the story of the reconstruction are on display around the back of **Il Duomo**. ⏱ *30 min. Entrance on Via Cavour. Daily 9:30am–1pm and 3:30–8pm. Admission €1.50 (free to Duomo).*

Il Duomo di San Nicoló, Noto.

Best Towns & Cities

6 ★ Palazzo Villadorata. On the far side of the Duomo, the now restored Villadorata Palace was once the residence of the princes of Villadorata, an 18th-century Spanish baronial family. It's crowned by six bulging 'goose-breast' balconies, each supported by sculpted buttresses of mythical monsters, snarling sphinxes, chubby-cheeked cherubs, and all manner of other beasts, both human and otherworldly. The interior, fully restored to its former glory, gives a taste of the opulence of Sicilian nobility, full of frescoes, majolica flooring, and sumptuous brocades. There are 90 rooms—the most beautiful being the Salone Rosso, Salone Giallo, and Salone Verde (the Red, Yellow, and Green Salons respectively). ⏱ *45 min. Palazzo Villadorata, Via Corrado Nicolaci.* ☎ *0931-835005. Admission €3. Tues–Sun 10am–1pm and 3–7pm. Note that opening times are subject to change.*

7 Piazza XVI Maggio. Stroll along the Corso until you reach this piazza, which is graced by the **Villetta d'Ercole**—a charming garden of monkey puzzle trees, palms, and an 18th-century **fountain of Hercules** that was rescued from Noto Antico. Just behind the fountain is the helpful **Tourist information office**. ⏱ *30 min. Piazza XVI Maggio.* ☎ *0931-573779. www. comune.noto.sr.it. Mon–Fri 8am–2pm and 3:30–6:30pm, Sat 9am–noon and 3:30–6pm. Reduced hours in winter.*

The 18th-century fountain of Hercules.

8 Chiesa di San Domenico (Church of St Dominic). Dominating the piazza and gardens is the recently restored Chiesa di San Domenico, which stands alongside a convent of the same name. Another masterpiece of the Baroque by Gagliardi, it has an especially beautiful façade, while the interior contains fine stucco work and attractive polychrome marble altars. ⏱ *20 mins. Chiesa di San Domenico, Piazza XVI Maggio. Free admission. Daily 8:30am–noon and 4–7:30pm.*

Where to **Stay**

★ **La Fontanella** JUST OUTSIDE THE HISTORIC CENTER On the northern edge of the old town, this former 19th-century palazzo has three stars. Rooms are pleasingly decorated in rustic style and some have balconies. It's about a 10 minute walk into town, and so conveniently placed and parking shouldn't be a problem. No restaurant, 'but plenty of dining options within a few minutes' walk. *Via Rosolino Pilo, 3.* ☎ *0931-894735. www.albergo fontanella.it.12 units. Doubles €60–80. AE, MC, V.*

★ **Villa Canisello** WEST OF CENTER This restored 19th-century farmhouse is an oasis of calm, set among lush vegetation in a quiet suburb. Bedrooms are on the small side, but well-presented, and each opens onto a terrace or patio. The bathrooms are shower only, and some rooms have ceiling fans while others have air conditioning. In spite of its quiet location, it's only a 15 minute or so walk to the historic heart of Noto. *Via Pavese 1.* ☎ *0931-835793. www.villacanisello.it. 7 units. Doubles €70–90. No credit cards.*

★ **kids Villa Mediterranea** LIDO DI NOTO Located just over 7km (4½ miles) to the southeast of Noto, this little hotel is on the seafront with its own gardens and a pool. It's a family-run, welcoming establishment with comfortable rooms, tiled floors, and bathrooms with shower only. There's also access to the hotel's private beach. *Viale Lido.* ☎ *0931-812330. www.villa mediterranea.it. 15 units. Doubles €80–150. AE, MC, V Open Apr–Oct.*

Where to **Dine**

★ **Il Barocco** HISTORIC CENTER Set off the Corso, in the former stables of a nearby *palazzo*, this is a charming and light-hearted find. There's tasty seafood (try the wonderful *fritto misto* (mixed fry-up), *al dente* pasta, and pizzas are available in the evening. The walls are plastered with graffiti—in the form of accolades for the eccentric and extrovert owner, Graziella. Dine under vaulted ceilings or in the charming courtyard. Reservations recommended. *Via Cavour, 8.* ☎ *0931-835999. Menus €12–25. MC, V. Lunch and dinner daily.*

★ **Trattoria Al Buco** HISTORIC CENTER A buzzing, modestly priced restaurant that's very popular with locals and also centrally positioned, just off the Corso Vittorio Emanuele. Fresh, simply prepared fish is the main staple, but vegetarians are also well catered for. The deep-fried, sunny zucchini (courgette) flowers are a delight. *Via G. Zanardelli, 1.* ☎ *0931-838142. Main courses €12–20. MC, V. Lunch and dinner Sun–Fri.*

Palermo

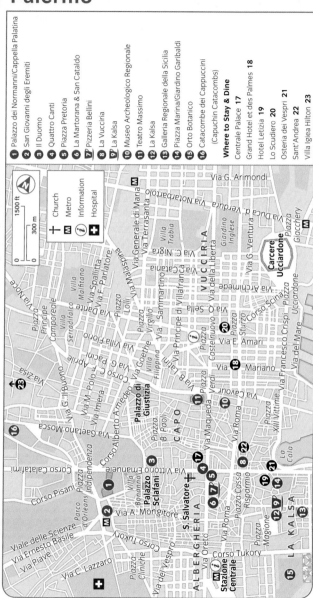

Notoriously the home of mafia assassinations, corruption, and organized crime, at first impression Palermo looks like a city with danger lurking on every corner. Yet despite its crumbling appearance and magnificent chaos, restoration is in the air, and a new flowering of this tantalizing capital is just beginning. The entire city is a treasure trove of Baroque buildings and museums and nowhere else on the island has such a splendid collection of Arab-Norman buildings. We love it.

① ★★★ **Palazzo dei Normanni/ Cappella Palatina.** The Palatine Chapel is Palermo's greatest architectural treasure—literally, the jewel in the crown. The interior is completely smothered in glittering 12th-century mosaics depicting biblical scenes, some of which are uniquely interpreted: Adam and Eve are shown with the forbidden fruit in their mouths and Eve is reaching for her second apple, and next to it are Islamic carvings of a picnic in a harem. Dominating the whole is Christ the Pantocrator in the cupola and apse. Built by Roger II as his private chapel (1132–43), it's a magical blend of different architectural styles. As John Julius Norwich wrote in *The Normans in Sicily*, it's a

Palazzo dei Normanni.

seemingly effortless fusion of all that is most brilliant in the Latin, Byzantine, and Islamic traditions into a single harmonious masterpiece'. The highlight of the Palazzo's Royal Apartments is the Sala di Ruggero II—King Roger's bed chamber—decorated with 12th-century mosaics of hunting scenes. ⏱ *2 hrs. Palazzo dei Normanni, Piazza Indipendenza, 1.* ☎ *091-7054317. Mon–Sat 8:30am–noon and 2–5pm, Sun 8:30am–2pm. Admission €6, including to La Cappella Palatina: Mon–Sat 8:30am–noon and 2–5pm, Sun 8:30am–9:45am and 11.45am–12:30pm.*

② ★ **San Giovanni degli Eremiti.** Just south of the Palazzo, this 12th-century church with its five red cupolas is one of the most famous

of all the Arab-Norman buildings and a distinctive landmark on the Palermo skyline. The small Norman cloister, overgrown with jasmine, bougainvillea, and citrus blossoms, was part of the original Benedictine monastery that once stood here. The church is closed indefinitely for restoration but this is still a romantic spot. *Via dei Benedettini 3.* ☎ *091-6515019. Closed for restoration.*

③ ★ **Il Duomo.** Palermo's cathedral has been reworked many times, but it remains famous as a fine example of the unique Arab-Norman style. Construction began in 1184 when the archbishop of Palermo, Gualtiero Offamiglio, vowed to rival the supremacy of the cathedral of

Monreale—and it became known as 'the battle of the two cathedrals'. The **Tesoro** (Treasury) has some sparkling exhibits, including a 13th-century jewel-encrusted golden crown, which was gifted to Constance of Aragon, wife of Frederick II. 🕐 *45 min. Il Duomo, Piazza di Cattedrale, Corso Vittorio Emanuele.* ☎ *091-334373. Free admission (donation appreciated). Mon–Sat 9:30am–1:30pm and 2:30–5:30pm; Sun 7:30am–1:30pm and 4–7pm. Treasury admission €2. Mon–Sat 9:30am–1:30pm, 2:30–5:30pm.*

4 Quattro Canti. At the intersection of Via Vittorio Emanuele and Via Maqueda, four ancient neighborhoods uncurl from the Quattro Canti (four corners) crossroads—the busy heart of Palermo—although it's often traffic-choked and blighted by centuries of grime. Overlooked on all sides by four haughty Baroque figures, the first tier of each is decorated with a fountain and statue representing one of the four seasons.

5 ★★★ Piazza Pretoria. In the heart of Palermo's most picturesque and notorious square stands the city's most spectacular fountain, **Fontana Pretoria**. Designed by the Florentine sculptor, Francesco Camilliani in the mid-1500s, it was originally intended for a Florentine villa and is adorned with 30 naked or near naked figures. Nicknamed the Fontana della Vergogna (Fountain of Shame), it caused a furor when it was first unveiled and the local nuns chopped off the protruding bits—the noses—of many of the nude men. The statues were recently restored and ornamental railings erected around the enclosure to protect them in all their unashamed glory. They look especially dramatic when floodlit at night.

6 ★★★ La Martorana & San Cataldo. These two ancient churches overlook the nearby Piazza Bellini. La Martorana was commissioned in 1143 by the Norman King Roger II. Originally built in the form of a Greek cross, when it became part of the Catholic Church in the 17th century much was changed and, unfortunately, many of the original mosaics were discarded. But

Palermo's Cathedral.

Fontana Pretoria.

the surviving 12th-century mosaics glitter with gold, created by the same Byzantine artisans who worked on the Cappella Palatina (see p. 123), The Campanile outside is the pinnacle of Palermitan Norman-Arab architecture. Next door, the tiny Church of San Cataldo is remarkable for its tomato-red Moorish domes. Built in 1154, the interior retains its original ascetic atmosphere. The only real embellishment is the glorious original mosaic floor. 🕐 *40 min. La Martorana. Free admission. Mon–Sat 9:30am–1pm and 3:30–7pm, Sun 8:30am–1pm. San Cataldo: admission €1. 9am–1pm, 3:30–7pm, Sun 8:30am–1pm.*

7 ★★ **kids** **Pizzeria Bellini.** Just by the churches, this is a great spot for a long, cool drink or a gelato on the terrace, or a tasty pizza in the upstairs restaurant. *Piazza Bellini, 6.* ☎ *091-6165691. $.*

8 ★★★ **La Vucciria.** This quarter, stretching from Via Roma to San

Sweet Delight

The sweet marzipan, frutta martorana, is named after the former Benedictine convent of La Martorana. Every convent in Palermo in the Middle Ages specialized in different kinds of confectionery, which was molded into vegetable and fruit shapes. Now every shape and style goes, including *minni di vergini* (virgins' breasts) and the rather dodgy—but nonetheless delicious—*fedde delle cancelliere* (chancellors' buttocks).

Domenico, takes its name from the corruption of the French word *boucherie* (butcher's shop) because of the meat on sale in the market. But, in fact, you'll find every comestible you can think of in the open-air **Mercato** (market)—bloody-muzzled wild hare hang next to leery-eyed squid and the plumpest tomatoes imaginable—an ideal place to stock up for a picnic. In the warren of surrounding streets, you'll also find pirated CDs and DVDs, fake designer bags, and a great selection of kitchenware and coffee-making goods. This is Palermo's oldest, most colorful, and promiscuous market. The gesticulations, singing, and lively banter of the Sicilian cast are as entertaining as any West End or Broadway show.

When in Palermo do as the Palermitans do and wander around the market while tucking into a typical hot snack called *pannelle* (chick-pea fritters sprinkled with lemon). ⏲ *40 min.*

La Kalsa. Try a cornet full of *babbaluci*—hot baby snails marinated in olive oil, garlic, and parsley. You'll find them on sale everywhere in this quarter.

10 ★★★ Museo Archeologico Regionale. Housed in a Renaissance monastery, this very impressive museum is stuffed with artifacts from Neolithic times to the Roman era. You'll find the highlights in the Sala di Selinunte, including the *metopes* (carved stone reliefs) unearthed at the temples of Selinunte (see Chapter 3, p. 53). They depict such great legends as Hercules and the Cretan Bull and the Rape of Europa. ⏲ *2 hrs. Piazza Olivella 24.* ☎ *091-6116805. Admission €6 adults, €3 children. Tues–Fri 8:30am–1:30pm and 2:30–6:45pm, Sat–Mon 8:30am–1:45pm.*

Tip

Piazza Olivella buzzes at night with bars and restaurants, while the Via Bara dell'Olivella is famous for its craft shops and puppet theater—well worth a visit on Sunday afternoons to keep both adults and children amused.

11 ★★ Teatro Massimo. This is not only the largest theater in Italy, but the third largest in Europe (after the Paris Opéra National and the

La Vucchiria, Palermo's oldest and most colorful market.

Staatsoper in Vienna) and is renowned for its perfect acoustics. It's famous, too, as the set of the climactic opera scene in *The Godfather: Part III*. Like so much of Palermo, its history has been anything but simple. Palermitan architect Giovan Battista Basile was commissioned to build the theater in 1875 to mark the Unification of Italy. Progress was slow but, when it finally opened in 1897, it became the stage for the opera world's most famous stars including Caruso, Callas, and Pavarotti. It was then closed 'temporarily' in 1974 for renovation, scandalously not re-opening until 1998 with a glittering production of Verdi's *Aida*. Take a guided tour of the theater, (rehearsals permitting) or treat yourself to a night at the opera for a bit of glamour—remember, the Sicilians love to dress up. 🕐 1 hr. Via Maqueda. ☎ 091-6053555. www.teatromassimo.it. Opera season runs mid-Nov to end June but other performances including concerts and ballets are staged at other times. Ticket prices vary. Box office open Tues–Sun 10am–3pm. Guided tours: €6; Tues–Sun 10am–2pm and 3–4pm.

Cloister of the Museo Archeologico Regionale.

⑫ ★★ **La Kalsa.** Originally a wealthy Arab quarter, then a notoriously dodgy one, this area is now getting the restorative attention it deserves. Right now, it's more chic than shabby, and is full of fascinating piazzas and restaurants as well as many aristocratic *palazzi* and churches. It lies at the sea end of **Corso Vittorio Emanuele** and stretches as far as the **Orto Botanico** in the southeast and **Via Roma** in the southwest. 🕐 40 min.

Shopping

As well as the **Vucciria** market (see p. 126), check out the **Capo** and **Ballarò** markets too, where there's much more on offer than just fruit and veg, such as household goods and convincing 'designer' watches and clothing. Near **Piazza Pretoria**, the **Via Calderai** is lined with artisanal outlets specializing in painted metalwork—an age-old Sicilian skill, noticeable in the traditional handcarts. And, for the sweet-toothed, head to **Mangia**, **Via Principe di Belmonte**, for *buccellati*—little pies full of candied fruit, or boxes of decadent *cannoli* (see p. 173). The main shopping streets are between **Teatro Massimo** and **Piazza Politeama** and, for designer fashions, just north in the fashionable **Via della Libertà** neighborhood.

Palermo After Dark

Just as in Catania—or any other big city in the world—the best advice is to stay away from dimly-lit streets and corners. But for the bright lights, you'll find that everyone heads out of town in the summer, to seaside Mondello (11km/7 miles) that's full of open-air discos. In Palermo itself, the night scene is quite sleepy, but for a bit of nightclub action **I Candelai** (Via Candelai, 65; ☎ **091-327151**) has live music and DJs at weekends. Also check out **La Cuba** (Viale Francesco Scaduto; ☎ **091-309201**) for a spot of 'alfresco' dancing to live music in lovely gardens with a cocktail in hand. You'll find, too, a handful of clubs in the newly fashionable northern side of town around the Viale Regionale Siciliana.

🔞 ★★★ **Galleria Regionale della Sicilia.** This is Palermo's best museum and Sicily's greatest gallery of regional art, housed within the Catalan-Gothic **Palazzo Abatellis**—an architectural treasure in itself. The collection spans the arts in Sicily from the 13th to 18th centuries. *Palazzo Abbatellis, Via Alloro, 4, just east of Piazza Giardino Garibaldi.*

Marina. ☎ *091-6230033. Closed for restoration at the time of writing.*

🔞 ★★★ **Piazza Marina/ Giardino Garibaldi.** Cool and shady, Garibaldi's Garden is graced with swaying palms, figs, and huge banyan trees. The busy piazza alongside was used by the Aragonese in the 16th century for

Catacombe dei Cappuccini.

glorious weddings and jousts, but it was also a shameful site of public execution. Once the headquarters of the Spanish Inquisition, the Palazzo Chiaramonte is the largest palace on the piazza—it's now part of the University of Palermo but sometimes opens for concerts and temporary exhibitions (☎ **091-334139**). After dusk, the piazza is very animated with outdoor tables spilling out from the restaurants and cafés. ⏱ *30 min. Giardino Garibaldi: Free admission. Open 24 hrs.*

⑮ ★★ **Orto Botanico.** This delightful 18th-century botanical garden is fringed with sphinxes and pavilions, and lavishly planted with such exotic and fragrant plants as bamboo, towering banyans (one of which is over 150 years old), cinnamon and coffee trees, magnolias,

petticoat palms, and pineapples. There's also an aromatic Mediterranean herb garden. ⏱ *45 min. Via Abramo Lincoln, 2b.* ☎ *091-6238241. Admission €4. Apr–Oct Mon–Fri 9am–6pm (till 5pm rest of year) and Sat–Sun 8:30am–1:30pm.*

⑯ ★★ **Catacombe dei Cappuccini.** In the most macabre of Sicilian style the labyrinthine catacombs of the Capuchin convent are full of deceased Palermitans. Over 8,000 mummified bodies—dried out by a secret liquor-draining process—dressed up in their best, hung on walls or lying in stacked glass coffins—apparently grin out at you: an unnerving and utterly extraordinary sight. ⏱ *30–40 min. Via Cappuccini, 1.* ☎ *091-6524156. Admission €3, free for under-18s. Daily 8:30am–1pm and 2:30–6pm.*

Where to **Stay**

★★ **Centrale Palace** QUATTRO CANTI   This former 17th-century palazzo blends antiques with stucco work, frescoes, thick carpets, and excellent service. The rooftop garden terrace is the perfect spot for a drink or breakfast while savoring the views across to Monte Pellegrino. *Corso Vittorio Emanuele, 327.* ☎ *091-336666. www.centrale palacehotel.it. 104 units. Doubles €200–273. AE, DC, MC, V.*

★★ **Grand Hotel et des Palmes** CENTRAL   A little tired nowadays, but an air of nostalgic glamour lives on in this legendary hotel, with its unexpectedly grand interiors. This is where Wagner wrote *Parsifal* and where in the 1950s Lucky Luciano—the *capo de capi* of the Cosa Nostra—notoriously attended a meeting of gangsters. *Via Roma, 398.* ☎ *091-6028111. www.hotel-despalmes.it. 183 units. Doubles €184–235. AE, DC, MC, V.*

★ **Hotel Letizia** LA KALSA   This pretty boutique hotel is a stone's throw from the atmospheric Piazza Marina. It's elegantly furnished with antiques, gilt mirrors, and Persian rugs. Some rooms have Jacuzzis in the bathrooms. Outside is a small sun-drenched courtyard. Note that there are five floors and no elevator—so plenty of stairs. *Via Bottai, 30.* ☎ *091-589110. www.hotel letizia.com. 13 units. Doubles €88–135. AE, MC, V.*

★★★ **Villa Igiea Hilton** ACQUA-SANTA, NORTHERN OUTSKIRTS   This hotel is the resort-of-choice for

Roof terrace, Centrale Palace.

Piazza San Francesco dining.

plutocrats, presidents, and princi-
pessi. Very stylish in a discreetly Art
Nouveau way, the villa is surrounded by jasmine-scented gardens overlooking the sea. There's a
swimming pool and tennis court.
Salita Belmonte 43, Acquasanta.
☎ *091-6312111. www.hilton.com.
120 units. Doubles €185–445. AE,
DC, MC, V.*

Where to Dine

★★ **Lo Scudiero** NEAR VIA LIB-
ERTÀ   This fashionable brasserie
specializes in regional, Sicilian recipes, and is very popular with locals.
Vegetarians are well-catered for
too. Reservations recommended.
Via Turati 7. ☎ *091-581628. Menus
€27–48. AE, DC, MC, V. Lunch and
dinner Mon–Sat. Closed two weeks
in Aug.*

★★ **Osteria dei Vespri** OFF VIA
ROMA   Tucked away in a little
piazza, this smart, atmospheric restaurant is prized for its creative Sicilian cuisine. The impressive wine list
features hundreds of vintages. Less
impressive is the occasionally slow
service. *Piazza Croce dei Vespri 6.*

☎ *091-6171631. www.osteriadei
vespri.it. Reservations recommended.
Menu €50; tasting menu (7 courses)
€75. AE, DC, MC, V. Lunch and dinner
Mon–Sat. Closed 1 week in Feb.*

★ **Sant'Andrea** VUCCIRIA   One
of the best books about Palermo,
Midnight in Sicily, was written in this
amiable restaurant by Australian
author, Peter Robb. Fresh fish from
the market is the specialty, along
with such divine desserts as black-
chocolate mousse. *Piazza
Sant'Andrea, 4.* ☎ *091-334999.
www.ristorantesantandrea.eu. Reservations recommended. Menus
€27–38. AE, MC, V. Dinner only,
Mon–Sat. Closed 14th–27th Jan.*

Ragusa

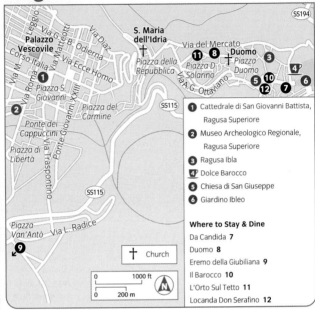

1. Cattedrale di San Giovanni Battista, Ragusa Superiore
2. Museo Archeologico Regionale, Ragusa Superiore
3. Ragusa Ibla
4. Dolce Barocco
5. Chiesa di San Giuseppe
6. Giardino Ibleo

Where to Stay & Dine

Da Candida **7**
Duomo **8**
Eremo della Giubiliana **9**
Il Barocco **10**
L'Orto Sul Tetto **11**
Locanda Don Serafino **12**

Church

0 ——— 1000 ft
0 ——— 200 m

Cicero's description of the Sicilian character as 'acute but suspicious and by nature polemical' doesn't apply in this gentle, quiet place of beautiful, honey-colored stone Baroque buildings. Here old-fashioned courtesy and friendliness are the norm. And now, with dozens of charming B&Bs and excellent restaurants springing up, it's also a center of gastronomic excellence.

Tip

If your time is limited, focus your visit on the old town—Ragusa Ibla—which is far more beautiful and intriguing than Ragusa Superiore (Upper Town), constructed as a new town after the 1693 earthquake, with wide streets laid out on a grid pattern. Bear in mind, however, that most of the shops and services are in the upper town.

1 Cattedrale di San Giovanni Battista, Ragusa Superiore.

This 18th-century Baroque cathedral is dedicated to St. John the Baptist with an ornate façade and soaring campanile. Inside it's a riot of gilding and stucco work and the Latin cross form has two orders of pillars, made from locally quarried asphalt. ⏱ *30 mins. Via Roma 134.* ☎ *0932-621658. Free admission. Daily 8:30am–noon and 4–7pm.*

Cattedrale di San Giovanni Battista, Ragusa Superiore.

② Museo Archeologico Regionale, Ragusa Superiore. The Regional Archeological Museum has well-displayed artifacts unearthed from the province, dating back to prehistoric times and including a 7th-century tomb carving *The Warrior of Castiglione*, as well as Greek vases,

Balcony, Ragusa Ibla.

Byzantine mosaics, and reconstructions of necropoli. 🕐 *40 min. Via Natalelli.* ☎ *0932-622963. Admission €3. Daily 9am–1:30pm and 4–7:30pm.*

③ Ragusa Ibla. The old town, gorgeously re-created as a Baroque city on a medieval street plan, takes its name from the Hyblaean (Ibla) Hills on which it rises. The best access is by the Santa Maria delle Scale stairway that affords panoramic views. The core is the **Piazza del Duomo** with the **Duomo di San Giorgio (St George's Cathedral)**. Its wedding-cake façade was the work of the celebrated architect Rosario Gagliardi from nearby Noto and is a splendid example of Sicilian Baroque. It's topped by a blue neo-classical dome—a landmark of the town. It was almost 40 years before its final completion in 1775 and, as St. George was regarded as the unofficial patron saint for the Sicilian aristocracy, this cathedral was traditionally patronized by the gentry and nobility. However, by contrast, the interior is rather plain. After sightseeing, treat yourself to a cooling ice cream or a typically Sicilian *granità* (crushed ice) at **Gelati di Vini** (Piazza del Duomo, 20; ☎ **0932-228989**; www.gelatidivini.it). Alongside all the old favorites, some are wine-flavored, others redolent of the freshest fruit, and others aromatic and nutty—but all are divine. ⏱ *30 min. Piazza del Duomo.* ☎ *0932-621779. Free admission. Daily 9am–noon and 4–7pm.*

4️ Dolce Barocco. Drop into this gelateria (ice cream parlor) and pasticceria (pastry shop) for a veritable feast—the signature dolce barocco ice cream is made to a secret recipe with hazelnuts, almonds, and carob fruit—all of which grow in profusion in this province. *Largo San Domenico.* ☎ *0923-655378. $.*

5️ Chiesa di San Giuseppe. Originally built in 1590, but badly damaged in the 1693 earthquake, the church's elegant façade and bulging balconies are the work of the Gagliardi school. ⏱ *20 min. Via*

Torre Nuova, 19. ☎ *0932-621779. Daily 9am–noon and 4–6pm, but hours variable.*

6️ ★★★ Giardino Ibleo. The Ibla Gardens are a perfect spot for a picnic or evening stroll, when all the locals join in for the *passeggiata*. The gardens offer terrific views of the surrounding mountains and valleys—some of the most scenic in all Sicily. Look out for the remains of several small churches within the grounds. The Church of San Giorgio Vecchio is near the park entrance, and although mostly in ruins, it still retains some elements of its original 15th-century Catalan-Gothic construction. Look too for the remains of the 14th-century Chiesa di San Giacomo with its painted ceiling by Pietro Novelli. And the Chiesa San Domenico is noted for its bell-tower decorated with ceramic tiles from Caltagirone. ⏱ *30 min. Ragusa Tourist Information. Via Capitano Bocchieri, 33.* ☎ *0932-221529. www.ragusaturismo.it. Giardino Ibleo is open daily 8am–8pm. Free admission.*

Where to **Stay**

★★ Eremo della Giubiliana

TOWARDS MARINA DI RAGUSA Halfway between Ragusa (14km (8½ miles) southwest) and the coast, this fortified farmstead and former convent once belonged to the Knights of Malta. Set among lush, walled gardens this is a peaceful retreat of discreet luxury and great architectural and antique charm. The rooms in the main building are stylishly appointed, while five cottages in the grounds are still rather 'new' but well-placed for the hotel's private airstrip, from where excursions to offshore islands and farther afield to

Malta can be arranged. *Contrada Giubliana.* ☎ *0932-669119. www. eremodellagiubliana.com. 18 units. Doubles €275–385. AE, MC, V. Closed 12th Jan–8th Feb.*

★★ Il Barocco IBLA Located near the Giardino Ibleo, this family-run hotel is decorated in apricot and terracotta tones, and set around a little courtyard. Inside the rooms are showcases for local artists with hand-painted murals of local scenes and elegant, classical furnishings set on cool, tiled floors. *Via Santa Maria La Nuova 1.* ☎ *0932-663105. www.*

ilbarocco.it. 14 units. Doubles €80–100. AE, MC, V.

★ **L'Orto Sul Tetto** IBLA This Pompeii-red townhouse is situated on Ibla's main (but not too busy) street. Elegance is married with homeliness in just three guest bedrooms and features include *maiolica* floor-tiles and stairs in a striking local black stone, *pietra pece.* Breakfast is served on the lovely garden terrace on the roof—*l'orto sul tetto*—from where the B&B takes its name—where the knowledgeable hosts will treat you to home-made delicacies. *Via Tenente Distefano, 56.* ☎ *0932-247785. www.lortosultetto.it.* 3 units. Doubles €70–90. No credit cards.

★★ **Locanda Don Serafino** IBLA In the heart of the old town, this atmospheric stone warren is simply but elegantly furnished. Rooms tend to be small so, if your budget allows, go for the roomier suites such as No. 6, which has great views as well as a large hot tub. *Via XI Febbraio, 15.* ☎ *0932-220065. www.locandadonserafino.it.* 10 units. Doubles €80–100. AE, MC, V.

Where to **Dine**

★ **Da Candida** IBLA A simple restaurant with no Michelin stars, Da Candida is nonetheless a very good and reasonable find, serving such scrumptious specialties as *ravioli di ricotta* in *sugo di maiale* (ravioli stuffed with ricotta in pork sauce). *Via Valverde, 95.* ☎ *0932-345612. www.ristorantedacandida. it.* Menus around €20. DC, MC, V. Open lunch and dinner Tues–Sun.

★★★ **Duomo** IBLA Chef Ciccio Sultano has been awarded two Michelin stars in this stylish, comfortable restaurant beside the Cathedral. Sultano's style of cuisine is extremely adventurous and creative. Expect cylinders of grilled vegetables, Ragusano cheese tartlets with marmalade of wild-hawthorn apples, and black spaghetti among the many delicacies. Try to leave room for mouthwatering desserts such as the sublime *cannolo Siciliano*—here interpreted with Ibla sheep's ricotta cheese and pistachios from the flanks of Mt. Etna. You need a reservation to eat at this temple of gastronomy—and deep pockets. *Via Capitano Bocchieri, 31.* ☎ *0932-651265. www. ristoranteduomo.it.* Menus €75–101. AE, MC, V. Lunch Tues–Sun. Closed Sun eve, Mon, 10 days in Jan, 10 days in July, and 19th–29th Nov.

★★★ **Locanda Don Serafino** IBLA This one-Michelin-starred restaurant is set in barrel-vaulted stone rooms where the upcoming young chef Vincenzo Candiano is a wizard with local, fresh ingredients. The home-made pasta is divine. Follow it with Nebrodi pork fillets in an exquisite sauce of Marsala and Modica chocolate. The wine cellar is exceptionally well stocked with over 1,000 labels. *Via Orfanatrofio, 39.* ☎ *0932-248778. www.locandadon serafino.it.* Menus €55–75. AE, MC, V. Open lunch and dinner Wed–Sun. Closed 2 weeks in Nov and 2 weeks in Jan.

Siracusa

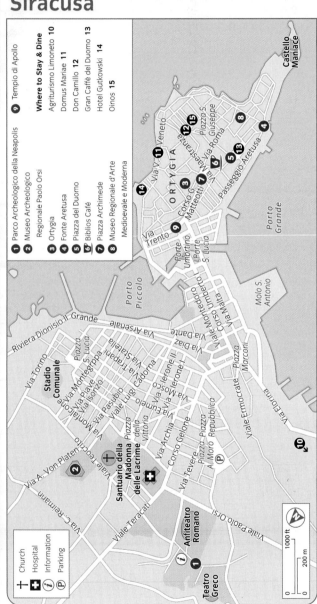

1 Parco Archeologico della Neapolis
2 Museo Archeologico
  Regionale Paolo Orsi
3 Ortygia
4 Fonte Aretusa
5 Piazza del Duomo
6 Biblios Café
7 Piazza Archimede
8 Museo Regionale d'Arte
  Medioevale e Moderna
9 Tempio di Apollo

Where to Stay & Dine
Agriturismo Limoneto 10
Domus Mariae 11
Don Camillo 12
Gran Caffè del Duomo 13
Hotel Gutkowski 14
Oinos 15

The Greeks always knew a good site when they saw one—and from the 5th-century BC Siracusa boomed as the Mediterranean's most powerful city. Here, Plato came to teach philosophy, Aeschylus to write his plays, and Siracusa-born scientist and engineer Archimedes rushed down the streets crying 'Eureka!'. The Roman orator Cicero later called it the most beautiful of all Greek cities.

❶ ★★★ Parco Archeologico della Neapolis. Located in the northwest of town, this is the site of an extraordinary number of well-preserved Greek and Roman remains, including the **Teatro Greco**—one of the great theaters of classical times, hewn from rock in the 5th century BC (see Chapter 3, p. 59). Outside the entrance are the old stone quarries (*latomie*) and the **Orecchio di Dionisio** (Ear of Dionysius), a vast ear-shaped grotto with cathedral-like acoustics, cut into the rock face, and so-named by the artist Caravaggio during his visit in 1608. The **Anfiteatro Romano** (Roman Amphitheater) is one of the top five theaters left by the Romans in Italy. Its function was quite different from the Greek version. Here gladiators did battle with wild animals in spectacles of blood-curdling violence. In the

Experience the acoustics at the Orecchio di Dionisio.

center is a rectangular tank, probably used as a drain for the gore and blood. ⏱ *2 hrs. Parco Archeologico della Neapolis, Via Teatro (off the intersection of Corso Gelone and Viale Teocrito).* ☎ *0931-66206. Admission €6. Tues–Sun 9am–7pm (closes earlier in winter).*

❷ ★★ Museo Archeologico Regionale Paolo Orsi. Just a stone's throw from the archeological park and named after the island's most eminent archeologist, this ultra-modern building contains one of the most important museums of its type in southern Italy and probably the finest archeological collection in Sicily. The dazzling array of artifacts ranges from skeletons of dwarf elephants to thousands of pottery fragments, burial urns, and amphorae. Divided into four sections, the most recently opened, section D has finds from Greek and Roman Siracusa including the splendidly sensuous statue of **Venus Anadiomene**. Look too for the **Sarcofago di Adelfia**—a sublimely crafted 4th-century marble tomb. ⏱ *2 hrs. Viale Teocrito, 66.* ☎ *0931-464022. Admission €6. Tues–Sat 9am–7pm, Sun 9am–2pm (reduced hours in winter).*

Tip

A joint ticket for the archeological park and the museum costs €10, which is a good saving. You could easily spend a whole morning in the museum and visit the archeological park in the afternoon.

3 ★★★ **Ortygia.** The tiny island of Ortygia (the historic heart of Siracusa) is linked to the mainland by a bridge. In Greek mythology it was said to have been ruled by Calypso, the sea nymph who detained Ulysses for seven years. Measuring only 1km by 500m, it's difficult to get lost and the best way to visit is by serendipity, on foot. Covering over 2,500 years of history, there's a huge variation of architectural styles from Greek to Roman remains and from Medieval-Norman to Baroque. In recent years, a lot of sensitive restoration work has been in progress, recapturing some of the island's former glory. ⏱ *1 day.*

4 ★★★ **Fonte Aretusa.** A short stroll along the western side of Ortygia (after crossing the bridge from the mainland) brings you to the celebrated **Fountain of Arethusa**.

Legend has it that the river god Alpheios fell in love with the sea nymph Arethusa, who fled underwater to Siracusa to escape his amorous advances. The goddess Artemis transformed her into this fresh water spring—but it was all in vain as Alpheios found her and 'mingled' his waters with hers. According to another legend, the spring ran red when bulls were sacrificed at Olympus. Nowadays, it's a lovely spot with ducks quacking among papyrus plants and plenty of well-placed waterfront bars and restaurants. ⏱ *30 mins. Via Picherali.*

5 ★★★ **Piazza del Duomo.** Said by many to be Sicily's most beautiful Baroque piazza, the centerpiece is undoubtedly the **Duomo.** Built on the site of a 5th-century BC temple to Athena. Extraordinarily, 26 of the temple's Doric columns are still visible. In its

View from the ramparts, Ortygia.

Fountain in Piazza Archimede.

heyday, a statue of Athena bearing a golden shield stood on the roof as a beacon to sailors miles away at sea. As a result of the 1693 earthquake the Norman façade collapsed and it was rebuilt in the Baroque style. The interior too is notable—for its ornate chapels and its Norman font, crafted from marble, inscribed in Greek, and supported by seven bronze lions. Also on this square is the beautifully symmetrical baroque **Palazzo Beneventano** and the church of **Santa Lucia all Badia**, the town's patron saint. ⏲ *30 mins. Duomo: Free admission. Daily 8am–noon and 4–7pm.*

⑥ **Biblios Café.** If you fancy a little read, a spot of coaching in the Italian language, or even a dance lesson to accompany your cappuccino or espresso, this bookshop is a cosy spot. At night, it also becomes a lively little bar. *Via del Consiglio Reginale, 11, Ortygia.* ☎ *0931-21491. $.*

⑦ **Piazza Archimede.** Known as the city's *salotto* (drawing room), this piazza is named after Archimedes, the town's most famous son. At its heart is the 19th-century **Fountain of Diana** (by Giiulio Moschetti, festooned with sirens and handmaidens, and flanked by Catalan-Gothic *palazzi* such as the 15th-century **Palazzo Lanza**—remarkable for its original Gothic windows. ⏲ *20 mins.*

⑧ **Museo Regionale d'Arte Medioevale e Moderna.** Set in the 13th-century Palazzo Bellomo, this museum is notable for its magnificent art collection spanning the Middle Ages to the 20th century. At the time of writing, it's closed for lengthy restoration. *Via Tempio di Apollo, Capodieci, 14.* ☎ *0931-69511.*

⑨ **Tempio di Apollo.** Set in the middle of a rather shabby square are the sunken remains of Sicily's oldest city temple, built in 656 BC and only discovered by chance in 1862. The inscription on the Doric temple says that it was dedicated to

Apollo, but after Cicero came to Siracusa, he wrote that the temple was dedicated to Artemis. 🕐 *20 mins. Piazza Pancali. Free.*

Tip

On entering the island turn left and this takes you to the colorful daily morning street market, which sells a tantalizing array of fruit, vegetables, fish, and meat, ideal for stocking up for a picnic. At the end of the market is a must-see for food lovers: the delicatessen 'I Sapori dei Gusti Smarriti' (literally 'the flavors of lost tastes'). Here you can find cheeses,

hams, and cured meats of the very best quality, together with a mouth-watering assortment of wines, condiments, sun-dried tomatoes, and other Sicilian delicacies made by the shop's owners in their 'laboratory'. For glorious scents, lotions, potions, and soaps visit the shop Ortigia (Via Maestranza, 12; ☎ 0931-461365). All their products are made from natural and traditional ingredients, such as olive oil, palm oil, almond oil, lanolin, naturally distilled lavender, and vegetable dyes—traditional products with a modern ethic.

Where to **Stay**

★★ kids Agriturismo Limoneto SOUTHWEST OF SIRACUSA   Cradled between mountains and sea (9km/5½ miles from Siracusa), this tranquil retreat set among citrus groves and orchards is a real joy. Rooms are comfortably furnished in rustic style and you dine in a

house-party atmosphere. Most of the food is home-grown and guests are invited to pick their own fruit. Different kinds of activity are on offer including archery and fitness classes. The farmhouse is also very convenient for visiting Ragusa and Noto. *Via del Platano 3, Contrada*

Agriturismo Limoneto.

Magrentino, access by SP14 direction Monte Mare. ☎ *0931-717352. www.limoneto.it. 10 units. Doubles €80–120. Dinner €20–30. MC, V. Free parking. Closed Nov.*

★ Domus Mariae ORTYGIA

Overlooking the waterfront, this is Siracusa's only hotel with its own chapel. Once a Catholic school, it's still owned by an order of Ursuline nuns. But there are no attempts to foist religious education on guests. This is a very pleasant small establishment with simple spotlessly clean rooms equipped with modern furniture. There's a peaceful reading room and a fine rooftop terrace for sunbathing. When booking, request a sea-facing room. *Via Vittorio Veneto 76.* ☎ *0931-24854. www.domus maria.eu. 12 units Doubles €150–165. AE, DC, MC, V. Free parking.*

★★ Hotel Gutkowski ORTYGIA

Set in a town house on the waterfront, this small welcoming hotel makes a virtue of its scaled-down style. Expect chic but utterly uncluttered rooms with tiled floors in the *arte povera* (poor art) type. Tasty breakfasts include freshly made juices and preserves. Reserve well in advance to clinch one of the four rooms with sea views. *Lungomare Vittorini 26.* ☎ *0931-465861. www. guthotel.it. 25 units. Doubles €85–110. AE, MC, V. Free parking in front of the hotel (subject to availability).*

Where to Dine

★★★ Don Camillo ORTYGIA

One of the city's finest restaurants, set in the vaults of a former 15th-century monastery. The freshest fish features, including sea urchins that are served to perfection here, and the catch of the day can be prepared to your order. The comprehensive wine list features more than 450 different wines. *Via Maestranza 96.* ☎ *0931-67133. www. ristorantedoncamillosiracusa.it. Reservations recommended. Menus €38–56. AE, MC, V. Lunch and dinner Mon–Sat. Closed Christmas.*

★ Gran Caffè del Duomo SIR-
ACUSA This café is the perfect spot for a drink or snack outside on the terrace overlooking what is arguably the most beautiful piazza in Sicily. They also serve superb ice creams and *cannoli* (sweet pastries) oozing with ricotta, if your tooth is sweet. Prices are extremely reasonable. *Piazza del Duomo, 18.* ☎ *0931-21544. Open all day. No credit cards.*

★★ Oinos ORTYGIA Situated in
the heart of the Jewish quarter, the young enthusiastic brigade here serve up creative delicacies that blend the best Piedmontese ingredients with Sicilian. The setting is designer-modern with an inviting terrace for eating *alfresco*. Classic Sicilian dishes such as *pasta con le sarde* (pasta with sardines) feature alongside more earthy, Piedmontese meat dishes. It's also a wine bar, and serves up tasty snacks. *Via della Giudecca, 69/75.* ☎ *0931-464900. www.ristoranteoinos.com. Reservations recommended for dinner. Menus €40–59. AE, MC, V. Lunch and dinner Mon–Sat. Closed 15th–28th Feb.*

Taormina

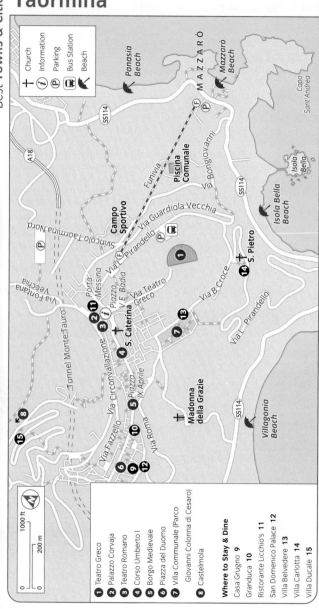

1 Teatro Greco
2 Palazzo Corvaja
3 Teatro Romano
4 Corso Umberto I
5 Borgo Medievale
6 Piazza del Duomo
7 Villa Comunale (Parco Giovanni Colonna di Cesaro)
8 Castelmola

Where to Stay & Dine

Casa Grugno **9**
Granduca **10**
Ristorante Licchio's **11**
San Domenico Palace **12**
Villa Belvedere **13**
Villa Carlotta **14**
Villa Ducale **15**

Perched on the side of steep cliffs with Mt. Etna as a back-drop, Sicily's most dramatic resort is almost picture perfect. The first tourist here was reputedly Goethe, in 1787, who waxed lyrical about the setting. Later D.H. Lawrence was just as enthused, describing Taormina as 'the dawn-coast of Europe'. Today, this beautifully preserved medieval town remains a magnet for writers, aristocrats, royalty, and film stars.

❶ ★★★ Teatro Greco. Tauromenion, meaning 'dwelling place on Mt. Tauro' in Greek, was founded in 358 BC by settlers who came from Naxos in the Aegean Sea, and this theater is the pinnacle of their achievement in Taormina. Apart from the one in Siracusa, this is the largest Greek amphitheater in Sicily. After the Greeks, there followed a roll-call of conquerors from Carthaginians to Romans, Saracens, French and Spanish. The remains of the Teatro Greco today are, in fact, virtually entirely Roman, dating from the 1st century AD. As so often happened with the Romans, the space was changed from a theater for dramatic plays to a gladiatorial circus—it became an amphitheater and huge cisterns were dug in the center. But nothing can diminish the setting with the coast and the menacing, fuming might of Mt. Etna as a natural backdrop. Because of the stunning setting and the excellent acoustics, the theater is used in the summer for theatrical shows, concerts, and films. 🕐 *1 hr. Teatro Greco, Via del Teatro Greco.* ☎ *0942-23220. Daily summer 9am–7pm, winter 10am–4pm. Admission €6, concessions €3.*

Tip

The Teatro Greco is Taormina's most visited sight—arrive early in the morning or toward closing time. Allow an hour to take in the views.

Teatro Greco, Taormina.

Climbing Mt. Etna

The extent to which you can explore Mt. Etna is always dictated by its activity. There are two points of access. Tickets are available from the northern **Piano Provenanza** for 4x4 minibus excursions to **Pizzi Deneri** (2,800m/9,186ft) or, activity permitting, to the main crater at 3,000m (9,842ft). You can walk from the top of each and round-trips last two to three hours, costing €44 and €60 respectively. Departures are at the operators' whim, but are usually hourly in the summer. Alternatively, take the **Funivia dell'Etna** (cable car) from the southern **Rifugio Sapienza**, a 4x4, and a guided walk (☎ **095-914209**; www.funiviaetna.com; daily 9am–4:30pm: total journey €48). Or ride the *funivia* (€27) and attempt the hike of up to four hours and return via the **Torre del Filósofo** (Philosopher's Tower) at 2,920m (9,579ft). When conditions permit, you can continue to the mouths of the steaming craters with a guide. Visibility is better in the mornings, but always be well-equipped for extreme mountain conditions.

❷ Palazzo Corvaja. At the bottom of Via del Teatro Greco, this 14th-century *palazzo* now houses the tourist information office. Up the staircase you come to the **Museo Siciliano d'Arte e Tradizioni Popolari**, a quirky collection of art and popular traditions embracing all kinds of folkloric items including painted carts, marionettes, oil portraits, and embroidery. ⏱ *30 mins. Tourist office, off Piazza Vittorio Emanuele.* ☎ *0942-23243. www.gate2taormina.com. Mon–Sat 8:30am–2pm and 4–7pm. Museo Siciliano d'Arte e Tradizioni Popolari: admission €3). Tues–Sun 9am–1pm and 4–8pm.*

Find Piazza IX Aprile for fantastic views across the coast.

Baroque fountain in Piazza del Duomo.

❸ Teatro Romano. On the other side of Piazza Vittorio Emanuele, behind the tourist office, are the ruins of the small **Teatro Romano** (Roman Odeon). Dating from the 1st century AD they were only brought to light in 1893, because they were partly covered by the church of **Santa Caterina** next door (daily 9am–noon and 4–7pm). You can see some of the excavations through the railings from the square before going into the church, where parts of the theater are exposed in the floor of the nave. A colonnade was also discovered here—perhaps the remains of a Greek temple dedicated to Aphrodite. ⏱ *20 mins.*

❹ ★ Corso Umberto I. This is Taormina's main, medieval street where everyone strolls, especially during *passeggiata* time at dusk. Flanked with bars, restaurants, and shops, it's always busy and provides a window on the world. For spectacular views, dive off into the utterly charming square, **★★★ Piazza IX Aprile**, roughly halfway along on the seaward side. Known as Taormina's 'balcony', there are magnificent panoramas from here across to the sea with Mt. Etna looming in the background. Savor the show from one of the bar terraces in the piazza. And take a look at the 17th-century façade of the Chiesa San Giuseppe, unusually embellished with skulls and crossbones, before taking a peek inside this very pretty

Villa Communale.

On the Tiles in Taormina

The evening passeggiata around the Corso Umberto I is like a stage set and there are plenty of spots nearby where you can savor the spectacle. The welcoming **O'Seven Irish Pub** (Largo Giuseppe La Farina, 6) just off the Corso is a great place for people-watching over a long, cool Guinness—or maybe a little fizzy white prosecco wine. For serious action, the **Panasia Beach** (Via Nazionale, Contrada Spisone; ☎ **0942-625195**) is a lido by day, but morphs into one of Taormina's hottest discos by night when all Sicily's gilded youth turns out to party—especially on Fridays until way past the first rays of dawn.

rococo church. ⏱ *1 hr. Piazza IX Aprile. Daily 9am–7pm.*

⑤ Borgo Medievale. The restored 12th-century **Torre dell'Orologio** (clocktower) at the western end of the Piazza IX Aprile is the gateway to the oldest part of the town, the **Borgo Medievale**. The Corso becomes narrower here and although there are still plenty of shops, they have kept their medieval character intact. ⏱ *30 mins.*

View from Castelmola.

⑥ Piazza del Duomo. The cathedral's eponymous piazza has an ornate 17th-century baroque fountain, the **Fontana del Tauro** with a two-legged female centaur—the symbol of Taormina. The **Duomo** (☎ **0942-23123**; daily 8am–noon and 4–7pm), was originally built in the 13th century. It has been extensively remodeled over the years and is currently closed for renovations. ⏱ *15 mins.*

⑦ Villa Communale (Parco Giovanni Colonna di Cesaro). Created by a Scot, Lady Florence Trevelyan, in the late 19th century, this park counts among the loveliest public gardens in Sicily. After a scandalous affair with Edward VII she was 'invited' to leave Britain, and came here and fell instantly in love with Taormina. As well as cypress, hibiscus, and magnolia trees there are curious pagodas and pavilions, vaguely reminiscent of Assyro-Babylonian style, which she built in her gardens. ⏱ *30 mins. Free admission. Daily dawn–dusk.*

⑧ ★★ Castelmola. Perched 5km (3 miles) above Taormina, this little hill village was founded by the Siculi people in the 8th century BC and is, simply, one of the most beautiful spots on the eastern coast. There

Wine

Sicily's luxuriant vineyards offer a wide choice and the wines were praised even in the days of Pliny (AD 23–79). Their flavor and strength have come to be appreciated by wine connoisseurs worldwide; Nero d'Avola is the robust black/ruby red wine of Sicily, while Bianco d'Alcamo is the classic crisp Sicilian white. The fertile flanks of Mt. Etna produce Etna Bianco (white) and Etna Rosso (red)—the first protected D.O.C. (*denominazione d'origine controllata*) to be awarded to Sicilian wines in 1968. Marsala, too, is famous for its fragrant wine, whether sweet or dry, and has D.O.C. status; the 10 year old Vergine Riserva is one of the world's finest, complex wines (see Chapter 3 for more on wine tours in Sicily).

are jaw-dropping views out to Mt. Etna and, if you're feeling especially energetic, a ruined castle stands at the highest part of the village, reachable by climbing the stairway from Piazza Belvedere. Several little bars and restaurants spill out onto the cobblestones, where you can sample Castelmola's delightful almond-flavored dessert wine (*vino alla mándorla*), either with a biscuit or just as it comes. ⏲ *1 hr.*

Tip

Taormina has no beach itself, but nearby Mazzarò has lovely pebbled coves (reachable by funivia from town) and Giardin-Naxos is well-endowed with long, sandy beaches. For more information see 'Best Beaches' in Chapter 4, p. 68.

Where to **Stay**

★★ San Domenico Palace
PIAZZA SAN DOMENICO (OLD NEIGHBORHOOD) One of Italy's greatest hotels. The guest list here reads like a Who's Who of celebrities and politicians. Originally a Dominican monastery, it's enclosed by walled-in terraced gardens, illuminated at night by flickering torches. The setting is spectacular, overlooking the sea and the guest rooms are beautifully appointed, many with antiques. The original part is in the old monastery, and the 'newer' wings were added in 1897, with more flamboyant furnishings.

Piazza San Domenico, 5. ☎ *0942-613111. www.santadomenico.thi.it. 105 units. Doubles €290–740. AE, CD, MC, V.*

★★ kids Villa Belvedere
GIARDINO PUBBLICO This friendly, family-run three-star hotel near the Public Garden offers the same views as more expensive hotels nearby. The rooms are nicely presented and those at the front are the best with sea views: the rooms at the very top have small terraces. There's also a splendid cliff-side terrace from where to savor the views and a swimming pool set in a lush,

San Domenico Palace Hotel.

flower-filled garden. *Via Bagnoli Croce 79.* ☎ *0942-23791. www.villa-belvedere.it. 49 units. Doubles €110–228. MC, V. Closed 16th Jan–19th Feb and 21st Nov–18 Dec.*

★★★ **Villa Carlotta** Set back from the San Domenico Palace, but enjoying the same spectacular views, this former family villa has been transformed into a gorgeous boutique hotel. The rooms are all are individually designed and elegantly furnished with spacious marble bathrooms, and there's a small outdoor swimming pool. Breakfast is a veritable feast of delights—served on the rooftop terrace. The hotel belongs to the same ownership as the Villa Ducale (below) and the staff are young, helpful, and very professional. A shuttle service runs to the beach. *Via Pirandello, 81.* ☎ *0942-626058. www.villa carlotta.net. 23 units. Doubles €150–320. AE, MC, V. Closed 15 Jan–15 Feb.*

★★★ **Villa Ducale** MADONNA DELLA ROCCA This restored villa is set in the quiet hamlet of Madonna della Rocca—between Taormina and Castelmola. The views over the sea, Mt. Etna, and the town are quite magnificent. Rooms are individually decorated in warm tones with terracotta floors and each room has a veranda. Breakfast and drinks are served on an outdoor terrace, from where you may even see the fiery glow of lava from Mt. Etna descending at night (as I did)—all from a very safe distance. The staff are charming and most helpful. There's a free courtesy minibus that will ferry you up and down into Taormina itself and a shuttle service to the beach. *Via Leonardo da Vinci, 60.* ☎ *0942 28153. www.villa ducale.com. 17 units Doubles €130–270. AE, MC, V. Closed 10th Jan–20th Feb.*

Where to **Dine**

★★★ Casa Grugno DUOMO   The Austrian-born chef Andreas Zangerl has won a Michelin star for this increasingly famous restaurant, which is the best in town. The setting is a Catalan-Gothic stone-sided former *palazzo* with a bar house that contains a bar, an ochre-colored dining room, and a courtyard terrace festooned with plants. Zangerl has his own take on traditional Sicilian cuisine, skillfully blending traditional dishes such as *pasta con le sarde* with more European offerings including suckling pig with wild fennel and beer. *Via Santa Maria de' Greci.* ☎ *0942-21208. www.casagrugno.it. Reservations essential. Menus €73–105. AE, DC, MC, V. Dinner Mon–Sat (also Sun in Aug).*

★ kids Granduca CORSO UMBERTO   In the heart of town, this restaurant is not only atmospheric but also serves excellent pizzas from the wood-fired oven in the evening. Other traditional Sicilian dishes such

as *spaghetti all Norma* are on the menu. On warm, balmy evenings, book ahead for a table on the terrace. *Corso Umberto I, 172.* ☎ *0942-24983. Reservations recommended. Menus €30–35. AE, DC, MC, V. Lunch and dinner Thurs–Tues.*

★ Ristorante Licchio's CORSO UMBERTO   In the historical center, just off the main drag, this buzzy restaurant specializes in seasonal cuisine, under the watchful eye of the charismatic owner Angelo. Start with an antipasto of fresh fish *carpaccio*, followed by *pasta fresca con le sarde* (fresh pasta with sardines), and then *filletto in salsa di Nero D'Avola* (beef fillet in Nero D'Avola wine sauce). The delicious home-made desserts include *cannoli* and *cassata*. In warm weather, ask for a table on the veranda. *Via C. Patricio, 10.* ☎ *0942-625327. www.licchios.it. Menus €25–30. MC, V. Open Fri–Wed lunch and dinner (also Thurs June–Aug). Closed 10th Jan–25th Feb.*

Ristorante Licchio's, Corso Umberto.

Erice

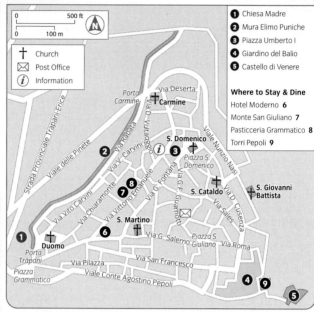

Legend:
- † Church
- ⊠ Post Office
- ⓘ Information

1. Chiesa Madre
2. Mura Elimo Puniche
3. Piazza Umberto I
4. Giardino del Balio
5. Castello di Venere

Where to Stay & Dine
Hotel Moderno **6**
Monte San Giuliano **7**
Pasticceria Grammatico **8**
Torri Pepoli **9**

Mystical Erice clings to lofty Monte San Giuliano. It was founded by the Ancient Elymians, worshippers of the fertility goddess Astarte—called Aphrodite by the Greeks and then Venus by the Romans. A temple dedicated to her stood atop the mountain, acting as a landmark to sailors. Today it's a beacon for visitors to stroll in the medieval streets, luxuriating in the stupendous views.

Tip

Erice has been called many other names—Eryx, Gebel-Hamed by the Arabs, Monte San Giuliano under the Normans—and only recently Erice, named by Mussolini in 1934.

1 Chiesa Madre. This 14th-century church lies just a stone's throw from the **Porta Trápani**, the medieval gate entrance to the southwestern edge of town. Its squat campanile was originally a watchtower built by

Frederick of Aragon (Frederick II of Sicily) and affords magical views across the Gulf of Trápani to the Egadi Islands. ⏱ *30 mins. Daily Apr–June and Oct 10am–6pm, July and Aug till 8pm, Sept till 7pm. Reduced opening during winter. Free admission (there's a modest admission charge to climb the tower).*

2 Mura Elimo Puniche. Walking north from the church, follow the Elimio Punic wall that skirts the northeastern side of Erice, constructed by the Elyminans between

Lifting the Veil

Frequently enveloped in mist, as it was in the days of Venus (or Aphrodite), the veils were nevertheless lifted in the temple where the cult of sacred prostitution was practiced. For centuries passing mariners took themselves in pilgrimage to her temple, all more than happy to be able to make a sacrifice to the goddess of love who, in return dispensed her voluptuous gratitude through the beautiful prostitutes who were sacred to her. Look for the immodest pose of Venus/Aphrodite in the fountain in the Giardino del Balio—the inspiration for the poet Giosuè Carducci's verses: 'From the shady Pelasgic topped by Eryx/There smiles and rules eternal Aphrodite./ And the coast blessed by her/Trembles all with love.'

the 8–6th centuries BC. The best-preserved section is along the Via dell'Addorata at the northern end of the fortifications. ⏱ *20 mins.*

3 Piazza Umberto I. The Via Vittorio Emanuele main route climbs steeply past shops to Piazza Umberto I—Erice's only large piazza—where you may be tempted to take a break in one of the cafés/bars. In this historic heart is the **Museo Civico Antonio Cordici**. Named after a local historian, its local artifacts from prehistoric to Roman times include a small head of Venus dating to the 5th century BC. ⏱ *40 mins Museo Civico Antonio Cordici, Piazza Umberto.* ☎ *0923-869172. Free admission. Mon–Fri 8am–2pm, also Mon & Thurs 2:30pm–5pm.*

4 ★★ Giardino del Balio. Head east to the gardens of Villa Balio on the summit of a hill. Named after a former Norman governor, the gardens were laid out in 1870. From here, you'll be treated to a patchwork of peaks, sea, saltpans, and in the distance the turtle-shaped Egadi Islands. If you're exceptionally lucky you may be able to see all the way to Tunisia's Cap Bon—a distance of

170km (106 miles). ⏱ *30 mins. Giardino del Ballo. Always open. Free.*

5 ★★★ Castello di Venere. A path winds from the gardens along the cliff edge to the Castle of Venus at Erice's highest point, on the spot where the temple once stood. Built in the 12th century, the remains of the *castello* are testimony to what was a huge and majestic defensive

The watchtower built by Frederick of Aragon.

Cobbled streets of Erice.

fortification by the Normans, encircled by medieval towers. Above the entrance you can see the coat of arms of Charles V and an original Gothic window. The views from here are even more unforgettable than those from the Giardino del Balio. 🕐 *40 mins. Castello di Venere. Free admission. Daily 9am–7pm, (but times are very variable).*

Where to **Stay**

The 12th-century remains of the Castello di Venere.

★ **Hotel Moderno** CENTRAL ERICE This centrally-located hotel is certainly modern in its well-equipped rooms with immaculate bathrooms, but it's also very charming and warm, furnished with some antiques and plenty of 19th- century stylish charm. During cold and misty weather, there's often a blazing fire. The hotel's restaurant is also highly regarded. *Via Vittorio Emanuele 63.* ☎ *0923-869300. www.hotelmoderno erice.it. 40 units. Doubles €95–120. AE, DC, MC, V.*

★★ **Torri Pepoli** UPPER TOWN ERICE Spectacularly set on a rocky crag with superb views, this original castle watchtower has been transformed into a charming and very exclusive small hotel. The five rooms and two suites are all individually furnished in neo-Gothic style, but with excellent modern comforts. The dining room is a fantasy of

Siculo-Arab style and the restaurant is highly acclaimed. *Viale Conte Pepoli.* ☎ *0923-860117. www.torri pepoli.it. 7 units. Doubles €150–350. AE, DC, MC, V. Closed 2 weeks in Jan.*

Where to **Dine**

★★ Monte San Giuliano PIAZZA UMBERTO I   Concealed in a garden with a well, this delightfully rustic restaurant specializes in fish and seafood served in the terraced garden and dining room. Seafood couscous is on the menu along with homemade pasta and countless other traditional Sicilian specialties. *Vicolo San Rocco 7.* ☎ *0923-869595. www.montesangiuliano.it. Reservations recommended. Menus €25–39. AE, DC, MC, V. Tues–Sun 12:15–2:45pm and 7:30–10pm. Closed 7th–25th Jan and 5th–23rd Nov.*

Pasticceria Grammatico VITTORIO EMANUELE   Maria Grammatico's world-famous café and pastry shop—where she sells *frutta di martorana* (marzipan fruits), *cudduredde* (fig biscuits), *crostate di marmellata* (jam tarts), *mostaccioli di Erice* (Erice cinnamon biscuits), and other delicacies. Maria was the subject of the book *Bitter Almonds Recollections and Recipes from a Sicilian Girlhood* by Mary Taylor Simeti. The book recounts the story of how, as a child, Grammatico lived in a cloistered orphanage in Erice

Doorway to the castle with coat of arms.

and learned how to make the beautifully handcrafted pastries that were sold to customers from behind a grille in the convent wall. *Via Vittorio Emanuele, 14.* ☎ *0923-869390.*

Marsala

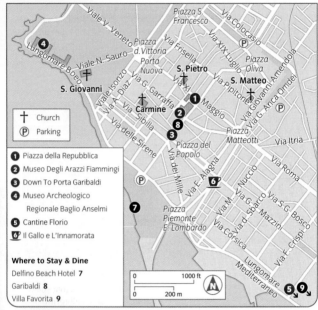

† Church

P Parking

1 Piazza della Repubblica
2 Museo Degli Arazzi Fiammingi
3 Down To Porta Garibaldi
4 Museo Archeologico
   Regionale Baglio Anselmi
5 Cantine Florio
6 Il Gallo e L'Innamorata

Where to Stay & Dine
Delfino Beach Hotel 7
Garibaldi 8
Villa Favorita 9

0   1000 ft
0   200 m

Proud Marsala is famous for its wine and its history. Exiled
from Mózia, the Phoenicians made it their stronghold, followed
by the Romans, and then the Arabs who named it Marsa Allah (Port
of God). In 1773, Englishman John Woodhouse arrived to make wine
rather than conquer. And it was here that Garibaldi landed with his
'Thousand' army, starting the Unification of Italy in 1860. Saluti!

1 Piazza della Repubblica.
Access to this main piazza in the historic heart of town is through the
great Renaissance monumental gate
Porta Nuova in the Western wall.
This is the site of Marsala's largest
church, the **Chiesa Madre** (Piazza
della Repubblica; ☎ **0923-716295**)
dedicated to St. Thomas à Becket,
the patron saint of Marsala. Originally
a Norman church, it was largely
rebuilt in the 1700s and again in the
20th century after its dome collapsed
in 1893. Decorated with statues and
flanked by two bell towers the

façade wasn't completed until 1956.
The rather cavernous interior is light-
ened by slender pillars and some
notable 16th-century sculptures by
the Gagini brothers. ⏱ *30 mins.*

**2 Museo Degli Arazzi Fiam-
mingi.** This museum has a collection of eight 16th-century Flemish
tapestries depicting scenes including the capture of Jerusalem from
the Saracens and the war fought by
Titus against the Jews in AD 66–67.
Hand-stitched in silk and wool, these
works of art were made in Brussels

between 1530 and 1550, and were gifted to the cathedral in 1589 by the Archbishop of Messina. ⏱ *30 mins. Museo degli Arazzi Fiammingi, Via Garraffa, 57 (entrance at the back of the Chiesa Madre).* ☎ *0923-712903. Admission €2.50. Tues–Sun 9am–1pm and 3–6pm.*

❸ Down To Porta Garibaldi.

From the Piazza della Repubblica, the main street Via XI Maggio is flanked by the town's shops and palazzi. The **Complesso San Pietro** has permanent exhibitions on Garibaldi, set in a restored former 16th-century Benedictine monastery. As well as Garibaldi's risorgimental history of the town, there are folkloric displays of popular traditions and also an interesting archeological section. Via Garibaldi continues south to the splendid gateway topped by an eagle, the **Porta Garibaldi**. ⏱ *40 mins. Complesso San Pietro, Via Ludovico Anselmi Correale.* ☎ *0923-718741. Free admission. Tues–Sun 9am–1pm and 4–8pm.*

❹ Museo Archeologico Regionale Baglio Anselmi.

Housed in a former Marsala wine warehouse, this fascinating museum's greatest treasure is the Punic warship that in all probability was sunk off these shores in 241 BC. Originally 35m (115 ft) long and manned by 68 oarsmen, it was thought to have been sunk during the First Punic War—where it lay in its watery grave until 1971 when it was discovered nearby in the Stagnone lagoon (near Mózia). This is the only known such war vessel ever to be uncovered. It's only part of the original ship, but this is a very clever, faithful reconstruction of how it would have looked. The exhibition also includes fascinating insights into life on board. ⏱ *1 hr. Museo Archeologico di Baglio Anselmi, Via Lungomare Boeo.* ☎ *0923-952535. Admission €3. Daily 9am–1:30pm and Wed, Fri, Sat and Sun 4–7pm.*

❺ Cantine Florio.

Established in 1833, the **Cantine Florio** is the best-known of the Marsala wineries where wines dating back to 1939 are still in maturation in the traditional tufa cellars. You can learn about the process of making Marsala, enjoy tastings, and of course buy from their well-stocked *enoteca.* One worth looking out for, despite the unappetizing name *Terre Arse* (meaning burnt lands in Sicilian), is a delicious, award-winning dry Marsala wine, good as an *aperitivo* or with cheese—wine experts enthuse over its 'nose of great finesse with hints of almond and toasted honey . . . with a noble background of liquorice and vanilla'. ⏱ *1 hr. Lungomare Florio,* ☎ *0923-781111. www.cantineflorio.it. Tours are available Mon–Fri, normally at 11am and 3:30pm, also 11am on Sat. Arrange English-speaking tours in advance by visiting the website, clicking on 'contacts' and filling out the form.*

Other wine cellars that you can visit are **Cantine Pellegrino** (Via del Fante 39; ☎ **0923-719911**); **Cantine Rallo** (Via Florio 2; ☎ **0923-721635**); **Donna fugata** (Via Lipari

Chiesa Madre, Piazza della Repubblica.

Sweet Nectar

The first man to popularize Marsala wine was British merchant, John Woodhouse, who came across the local brew in 1773. He was very partial to it and thought it could become popular back in England. He began to fortify it with alcohol so that it would survive the long ocean voyage. He was right and he soon moved to Marsala to begin mass production to satisfy the seemingly insatiable demand back home. He was followed by several other Brits, including Ingham and Whitaker.

18; ☎ **0923-724206**); and **De Batoli Marco e C.** (Contrada Samperi; ☎ **0923-962093**).

6 **Il Gallo e L'Innamorata.** A member of the Slow Food Movement this is a great little restaurant for savoring Sicilian specialties,

especially fish. But leave room for delectable desserts including testa di turco ('head of Turk')—a tasty treat of puff pastry and lemony blancmange that's a great feature of western Sicily's cuisine. *Via Stefano Bilardello, 18.* ☎ *0923-1954446. $$.*

Where to **Stay & Dine**

★ **kids** **Delfino Beach Hotel**
SOUTH OF MARSALA   Overlooking a sandy beach just under 5km (3 miles) south, this resort-style hotel is set behind a neo-Baroque façade. The rooms are decorated in bright, sunny colors with all modern facilities. Outside there are attractive gardens and a swimming pool. *Via Lungomare Mediterraneo 672.* ☎ *0923-751072. www.delfinobeach.com. 90 units. Doubles €80–130. AE, DC, MC, V. Amenities: restaurant, bar.*

★ **Garibaldi** HISTORIC CENTER
A member of the Slow Food Movement, this traditional trattoria near the Cathedral is especially noted for its wide selection of *antipasti*. There's an extensive list of well-priced Sicilian wines as well as, of course, Marsalas—sweet, dry, and every variation in between.

Piazza dell'Addolorata 35. ☎ *0923-953006. Menus €20–30. MC, V. Mon–Fri noon–3pm and 7:30–10pm, Sat 7:30–10pm, Sun noon–3pm.*

★★ **Villa Favorita** MARSALA OUTSKIRTS   Set in its own gardens, 2km (1½ miles) north of town, this elegant villa has retained much of its original character. The rooms in the main building are traditional with oak floors and loggias opening onto a courtyard. The garden rooms are whitewashed and are more simply decorated with direct access to the attractive gardens and swimming pool. The restaurant is good value. *Via Favorita 27 (off SS115 direction Trápani).* ☎ *0923-989100. www.villa favorita.com. 29 bungalows, 13 units (in the main building). Doubles €100–125. Double in bungalow €85–105. AE, DC, MC, V. Free parking.* ●

The
Savvy Traveler

Before You Go

Government Tourist Offices

Acireale: Via Scionti. ☎ 095-891999. www.acirealeturismo.it.

Aeolian Islands (Isole Eolie), Corso Vittorio Emanuele, 202, Lipari. ☎ 090-9880095. www.aasteolie. info & www.isole-eolie.com.

Agrigento: Viale della Vittoria, 255. ☎ 0922-401352. www.apt. agrigento.it.

Caltagirone: Via Volta Libertini, 4. ☎ 0933-53809. www.comune. caltagirone.ct.it.

Catania: Via Cimarosa, 10. ☎ 095-7306233. www.apt.catania.it.

Cefalù: Corso Ruggiero, 77. ☎ 0921-421050. www.cefalu-tour. pa.it.

Egadi Islands: Piazza Madrice, 8, Favignana. ☎ 0923-921647. www. egadiweb.it/proloco.

Enna: Via Roma, 413. ☎ 0935-528228. www.apt-enna.com.

Erice: Via Agostino Pepoli, 11. ☎ 0923-869388. www.proloco valderice.it.

Giardini-Naxos: Via Lungomare, 20. ☎ 0942-51010. www.aast@naxos.it.

Marsala: Palazza Vll Aprile, (off Piazza Repubblica). ☎ 0923-714097. www.apt.trapani.it (for Trápani province).

Mazara Del Vallo: Piazza Santa Veneranda, 2. ☎ 0923-941727. www.apt.trapani.it (for Trápani province).

Messina: Via Calabria, isolato 301 bis. ☎ 090-640221. www.apt messina.it.

Milazzo: Piazza Caio Duilio, 20. ☎ 090-9222865. www.aast milazzo.it.

Módica: Corso Umberto I, 149. ☎ 0932-753324. www.comune. modica.rg.it.

Noto: Piazza XVl Maggio. ☎ 0931-573779. www.noto@apt-siracusa.it.

Palermo: Piazza Castelnuovo, 34.

☎ 091-6058351. www.palermo tourism.com.

Piazza Armerina: Via Cavour, 15. ☎ 0935-680201. www.piazza-armerina.it.

Ragusa: Via Capitano Bocchieri, 33. ☎ 0932-621421. www.ragusa turismo.it.

San Vito Lo Capo: Via Savoia, 57. ☎ 0923-972464. www.comune. sanvitolocapo.tp.it.

Sciacca: Via Vittorio Emanuele, 84. ☎ 0925-84121. www.azienda turismosciacca.it.

Selinunte: Entrance to Parco Archeologico. ☎ 0924-46251. www.aptselinunte@micso.net.

Siracusa (Syracuse): Via Mae-stranza, 33. ☎ 0931-464256. www. apt-siracusa.it.

Taormina: Piazza Santa Caterina (Palazzo Corvaja). ☎ 0942-23243. www.gate2taormina.com.

Trápani: Piazza Scarlatti. ☎ 0923-29000. www.apt.trapani.it.

When to Go

As regards the weather, **April** to **June** and **mid-September** to **October** are the best months for a trip to Sicily. In **April** the island is ablaze with wild flowers and on the coast the first swimmers put their toes in the water, although sea tempera-tures can still be very bracing at this time. If **Easter** falls in April, it is well worth trying to coincide with one of the festivals celebrated at this time—combining tradition and folk-lore in spectacular processions and parades with music, feasting, and drinking. By **May,** temperatures on the coast should be warm with balmy evenings. Inland, the hills and mountains are carpeted with wild herbs and the mild temperatures make it ideal for walking.

SICILY'S AVERAGE DAILY TEMPERATURE

COAST	JAN	FEB	MAR	APR	MAY	JUNE
Max Temp. (°C)	11	13	15	17	21	27
Min Temp. (°C)	4	5	6	9	11	13

	JULY	AUG	SEPT	OCT	NOV	DEC
Max Temp. (°C)	30	30	26	20	15	12
Min Temp. (°C)	15	16	14	11	7	5

MOUNTAINS	JAN	FEB	MAR	APR	MAY	JUNE
Max Temp. (°C)	6	9	11	14	17	21
Min Temp. (°C)	−5	−4	0	4	6	7

	JULY	AUG	SEPT	OCT	NOV	DEC
Max Temp. (°C)	24	25	20	12	10	6
Min Temp. (°C)	10	12	10	6	3	−2

Summer arrives in **June** along with the strong, bleaching rays of the sun and the sea is now warm, although the beaches tend still to be deserted until the weekends. Now is also the perfect time for walking in the higher mountains and for indulging in the new crops of cherries and plums. The hottest, invariably crowded months are **July** and **August**, when the sea becomes the magnet for Sicilians and visitors alike, and everyone escapes from the sizzling heat of the cities, especially during the month of August. Yet, there are still many pleasures to be enjoyed. This is the time of year when cooling watermelons are in season and fig and peach trees are heavy with fruit. Around Trápani the salt is harvested from the salt pans and the vendemmia (grape harvest) gets underway towards the **end of August.**

By **mid-September** temperatures remain high and most of the crowds have left the beaches; **autumn** is approaching and with it many traditional food feste (festivals) are celebrated. At this time and in **October** there can be coastal storms, accompanied by high winds

and the suffocating North African scirocco wind, and seasonal rainfalls are now beginning.

From the **end of October** to **Easter** most attractions reduce their opening hours, many resorts become like ghost towns, and hard-working hoteliers and restaurateurs take time off. Yet, even in **November**, daytime temperatures can still reach the high 20°Cs (high 70°Fs), but this is also the time of the highest rainfall and it can get cool at night. In the deep **midwinter**, temperatures can still hover around 10°C (50°F) on the misty coasts, but the mountains are now cold and probably covered in a thick blanket of snow—much to the delight of skiers and snowboarders on Mt. Etna and the Madonie and Nebrodi mountains, for whom it's a winter playground.

Festivals, Special Events, & Public Holidays

Whatever the season, there's bound to be some kind of festival or event that coincides with your visit to Sicily. Every town has its own patron saint, but as well as the many religious festivals there are food feste, carnivals, and cultural events galore. The main holidays, a mix of religious and the secular, include: New Year's Day (Anno Nuovo)—celebrations on New Year's Eve (Capodanno). Epiphany (Befana) 6th Jan; Easter (Pasqua)— Good Friday & Easter Monday; Liberation Day 25th Apr; Labor Day 1st May; Republic Day 2nd June; Ferragosto (Feast of the Assumption) 15th Aug; All Saints' Day 1st Nov; Feast of the Immaculate Conception (Concezione Immaculata) 8th Dec; Christmas Day (Natale) 25th Dec; Boxing Day (Festa di Santo Stefan) 26th Dec. For more information on the following, call one of the tourist offices listed above on p. 158.

JANUARY. Befana (Epiphany)

Piana degli Albanesi (Plain of the Albanians). Located 29km (18 miles) from Palermo, this is a parade of residents in traditional Albanian costumes, climaxing in a firework display (☎ 091-8574144 or go to www.pianalbanesi.it). 6th January.

FEBRUARY. Carnevale, (Carnival). Literally, 'farewell to meat' during the week before Ash Wednesday, when towns all over the island erupt into parades and feasting before Lent begins. The carnival at **Sciacca** is especially famous for its spectacularly adorned floats, many of which satirize current events or figures of popular culture. Times vary according to Easter.

Feast of Saint Agata, Catania. Spectacular processions and feasting in which the silver reliquary of the martyred patron saint of Catania is carried through the streets. The event is witnessed by around a million people. 3–5th February.

MARCH/APRIL. Pasqua (Easter). Processions and passion plays mark Holy Week throughout the island. The most famous is **Trápani's**

four-day festival culminating in the slow procession of life-size *Misteri* (wooden statues).

MAY. Infiorata (Flower Festival), Noto. The residents of this little southeastern town celebrate the arrival of spring by decorating the streets and floats with flower petals, followed by dances and parades. Third Sunday in May.

JUNE. Festival of Greek Classical Drama. In Siracusa, Greek tragedies are performed in Italian by some of Italy's top actors in the only school of Classical Greek drama outside Athens. ☎ 0931-483378, Palazzo Greco, Ortygia. May & June. www.indafondazione.org.

JULY. The Feast of Santa Rosalia, Palermo. The relics of the patron saint of Palermo are paraded on a huge cart drawn by horses through the streets of the capital and there are torchlit processions to the saint's shrine on Monte Pellegrino, amid feasting and fireworks. 10–15th July.

Taormina Arte. The arts festival in Taormina showcases theater, concerts, and films by international names in a spectacular setting. www.taormina.arte. July and August.

AUGUST. Ferragosto (Assumption Day). The national holiday virtually shuts down the whole island, marking the event where Mary was said to have been 'taken up and assumed into heaven'. The festival is at its most colorful in Palermo. 15th August.

Palio dei Normanni (Horse Race of the Normans), Piazza Armerina. This medieval pageant celebrates Count Roger's capture of the town from the Saracens in 1087 with parades and feats of equine and rider dexterity in a thrilling joust. 13–14th August.

SEPTEMBER. International Couscous Festival, San Vito Lo Capo.
An annual couscous competition, staged outside Trápani, which attracts the world's best chefs—with ample tastings for everyone and plenty of dancing to live music to work it all off. three days in mid-September.

NOVEMBER. Ognissanti/Festa dei Morti (All Souls Day/Day of the Dead). Celebrated all over Sicily as a national holiday, it is a sort of local equivalent of Halloween, but rather more religious in flavor, when people pay homage to their dearly departed. A lot of sticky sugar figurines (*pupe*) are devoured. 1st November.

Getting **There**

By Plane

Most visitors fly first to Milan or Rome, and then take a connecting flight to Sicily, most often using Palermo or Catania as the gateway to the island.

Sicily's two main airports are **Falcone-Borsellino** (☎ 091-7020409; www.gesap.it) west of Palermo and **Fontanarossa** (☎ 095-340505; www.aeroporto.catania.it) serving Catania. There is also an international airport at Trápani, which has flights to and from some European cities.

Airlines Flying To/From Sicily:
Alitalia ☎ 022-314181 www.alitalia.com
Air Malta ☎ 091-6255848 www.airmalta.com
Air One ☎ 199-207080 www.flyairone.it
British Airways ☎ 199-712266 www.britishairways.com
Easyjet ☎ 0905-8210905 www.easyjet.com
Lufthansa ☎ 066-5684004 www.lufthansa.com
Meridiana ☎ 199-111333 www.meridiana.it
Ryanair ☎ 899-899844 www.ryanair.com
Tunis Air ☎ 091-6111845 www.tunisair.com
Volare ☎ 199-414500 www.volareweb.com
From North America: Flying time to Rome from New York, Newark,

or Boston is 8 hours; from Chicago, 10 hours; and from Los Angeles, 12½ hours. Flying time to Milan from New York, Newark, or Boston is 8 hours; from Chicago, 9¼ hours; and from Los Angeles, 11½ hours. There is also a new seasonal service by Eurofly (in partnership with Meridiana airline, see above) running direct flights between New York and Palermo twice a week in high season.

American Airlines (☎ 800/433-7300; www.aa.com) has regular services from New York to Milan and Rome.
Continental (☎ 800/525-0280; www.continental.com) has services from Newark to Milan and Rome.
Delta (☎ 800/221-1212; www.delta.com) flies from New York to Milan, Venice, and Rome.
Air Canada (☎ 888/247-2262; www.aircanada.ca) flies Toronto to Rome.

By Train

This is a convenient, although clearly slower, way to reach Sicily from the Italian mainland. Trains with connections from all over Europe, including Rome and Naples, arrive at the port of Villa San Giovanni, near Reggio di Calabria, in southern Italy. High-speed trains have made travel between France and Italy much faster in recent years. The service from Rome to

Palermo takes about 11 hours, while from Rome to Messina it's around 9 hours. If traveling from Europe, contact **Rail Europe Travel Centre** ☎ 08708 371371 (from the UK), www.raileurope.co.uk, or **Italian Railways,** ☎ 848-888088, www. trenitalia.com. For comprehensive rail information, visit www.seat61. com.

By Boat & Ferry

There are good sea links to mainland Italy. The major connection is from Villa San Giovanni in Calabria across the straits and over to Messina, in the northeast (12km/7½ miles). You can also reach Sicily from the Italian ports of Genoa, Livorno, Naples, and Cagliari (Sardinia), and from Tunisia and Malta. Rates vary dramatically according to season and crossings should be booked weeks in advance if you're planning to travel in high season. Check schedules, fares, and book

tickets at www.directferries.co.uk or www.viamare.com.

By Bus

Not surprisingly, there is no direct service to the island outside Italy. But, when in Rome, you could make the trek in 12 hours to Palermo—or 11 hours to Syracuse—with **Segesta** (☎ 06-4819676; www. interbus.it).

Passport & Visas

You require a full passport or national ID card to visit Italy from the UK and other EU states. Non-EU residents should also check visa requirements with the local foreign office.

Health requirements

There are no compulsory health formalities for visiting Italy.

For more detailed information specific for citizens of your country, please check the link to your foreign office.

Getting **Around**

Seeing the major sights of Sicily by public transport is entirely possible and, being among the cheapest in Europe, it's also very cost-effective. But trains don't run like clockwork and can be slow, and although buses can be a more reliable option, they don't run on Sundays. In addition, buses are usually more expensive than the train. A car gives you the most flexibility and, generally, the roads are good: but you must also be prepared for considerable chaos, especially in towns. Bring your nerves of steel!

By Air

There are domestic flights to Pantelleria and the Pelagie islands (close to Tunisia) from Trápani or Palermo for as little as €40 one-way. Check

the websites for **Meridiana** (www. meridiana.it) and **Air One** (www.fly airone.it) for timetables and offers.

By Train

All the major cities have rail links and, although using trains can be slow, it's generally an efficient and very affordable way to travel. The train service is usually better on the east side of the island than the west. Trains are operated by the state-owned **Trenitalia.** Call ☎ 848-888088 (or try www.trenitalia.it) for general timetable information and also where to book tickets. There is only one private railway in Sicily, the **Ferrovia Circumetnea** (☎ 095-541250; www.circumetnea.it), which is 110km (68½ miles) long. It starts from Catania and circles the base of Mt. Etna in a very scenic ride. Remember always to validate your train ticket before you ride. There are yellow machines installed at the entrance to all the platforms—you simply insert your ticket for it to be stamped. Failure to do this can cost you an instant fine.

By Bus

Where trains don't go buses, often do. But, depending on the destination, they may operate at limited times tied to school or market times.

The major bus company is **SAIS** (☎ 091-616028 in Palermo or ☎ 095-536168 in Catania; www.saisautolinee.it) offering services from Palermo to Messina, Catania, and Syracuse. **Cuffaro** (☎ 091-6161510; www.cuffaro.info) links Palermo in the north with Agrigento in the south. **Interbus** (☎ 094-2625301; www.interbus.it) has services between the cities of Catania, Messina, Taormina, and Syracuse. City buses are usually reliable and frequent, tickets for which must be bought before boarding and validated as soon as you hop on, otherwise you risk a fine. Buy your tickets at newsstands, ticket booths, or tabacchi (tobacconists). Most city buses charge a flat fare of €1.05 for a ticket that is valid for up to two hours. Some cities offer a 24-hour transit ticket that can save you money if you plan to use the bus network extensively.

By Car

You need a valid driving license, and if you are a non-EU license holder, an international driving permit. In the US, you can apply for an International Driver's License at any AAA branch. You must be at least 18 and have two 2x2-inch photos and a photocopy of your US driver's license with your AAA application form. The actual fee for the license

can vary, depending on where it's issued. Remember that an International Driver's License is valid only if physically accompanied by your original driver's license and only if signed on the back. To find the AAA office nearest you, call ☎ 800/222-4357 or 407/444-4300, or go to www.aaa.com. In Canada, you can get the location of the Canadian Automobile Association office closest to you by calling ☎ 800/267-8713 or going to www.caa.ca.

Car Hire: For sheer convenience and freedom, renting a car is usually the best way to explore the island. But you have to be a pretty aggressive and alert driver who won't be dismayed by super-high speeds on the autostrada (highway) or by narrow streets in the cities and towns. Sicilian drivers have truly earned their reputation as bad and daring. That said, your experience will be greatly enhanced if you take the decisive approach and demonstrate clearly where you're going by using indicators, using your horn liberally, and keeping your sense of humor. It is generally cheaper to make arrangements for car rentals before you leave home through a fly/drive deal. Of course, you can also rent a car once you arrive in Sicily. To do so, you need a valid passport and must be (in most cases) more than 23 years old. Insurance is compulsory and you would be wise to take out fully comprehensive insurance to cover you for any scrapes that are likely to occur. Prices vary dramatically, according to company, size of car, and even season—so do shop around.

The main rental agencies in Sicily include:
Avis (☎ 800/331-1212 (toll-free from USA/Canada); 08700-100287 (from UK); 091-591684 (from Palermo airport); www.avis.com).
Hertz (☎ 800/654-3131 (toll-free from USA/Canada); 08455-191536

(from UK); 095-341595 (in Catania); www.hertz.com).

The major Italian car-rental firm is **Maggiore,** (☎ 095 536927 (in Catania).

Gasoline: Known in Sicily as benzina, it is expensive for those accustomed to North American prices and in today's uncertain economy prices can change literally from day to day. Unleaded gas is called benzina senza piombo and diesel is gasolio. There are plenty of gas stations in and around towns, but if you're off the beaten path and especially on a Sunday, when many smaller stations are closed, it makes sense not to let your tank get too low.

Driving Rules: The Italian Highway Code follows the Geneva Convention, and Sicily, like the rest of Italy, uses international road signs. Driving is on the right; passing is on the left. Violators of the highway code are fined; serious violations may be punished by imprisonment. Random breath tastes are now regularly made in Sicily. The blood-alcohol limit is 0.05%: if you're involved in an accident while under the influence of alcohol, penalties can be very severe. In cities and towns, the speed limit is 50kmph (31 mph). For all cars and motor vehicles on main roads and local roads, the limit is 90kmph (56mph). For the autostrade, the limit is 130kmph (81 mph). Use the left lane only for passing. If a driver zooms up behind you on the autostrada with his or her lights on, that's your sign to get out of the way. Use of seat belts is compulsory.

Breakdowns & Assistance: The **Automobile Club Italiano (ACI)** does not offer free roadside emergency help to stranded motorists in Sicily. If you call the ACI emergency number (☎ 803-116) in the event of a breakdown, you must pay a minimum of €110 plus another around €45 to have your car towed to the nearest garage, plus tax and mileage charges. So getting stranded in Sicily has a hefty price-tag. Not only that, but 20% is added to the bill between 10pm and 6am and on Saturday and Sunday. ACI offices are at Via delle Alpi 6, in Palermo (☎ 091-300468; www.aci.it) and at Via Sabotino 1, in Catania (☎ 095-533380).

Sicilian Roads: The autostrada doesn't exist as extensively on Sicily as on the Italian mainland. The most traveled route is the A19 between Palermo and Catania, a convenient link between the island's two major cities. The other well traveled route is A20 going between Palermo and Messina. A18 links Messina and Catania on the eastern coast, whereas A29 goes from Palermo to the capital of the western coast, Trápani. Unless you're traveling from main city to main city, you'll use the Strade statali (state roads)—single-lane, toll-free routes.

Fast **Facts**

AMERICAN EXPRESS Travel agencies representing AmEx are found in large cities, including **La Duca Viaggi**, Viale Africa 14, in Catania (☎ 095-7222295); **La Duca Viaggi**, Via Don Bosco 39, in Taormina (☎ 0942-625255); and **Giovanni**

Ruggierie Figli, Emerico Armari 40, in Palermo (☎ 091-587144).

BUSINESS HOURS Regular business hours are generally Monday to Saturday from 8 or 9am to 1pm and 4 to 7 or 8pm. The riposo (mid-afternoon closing) is observed in Sicily. If you're on the island in summer, when the heat is intense, you too may want to learn the custom of *riposo*, retreating back to your hotel for a long nap during the hottest part of the day. Banking hours vary from town to town, but in general are Monday to Friday 8:30am to 1:20pm and 3 to 4pm.

CLIMATE   See 'When to Go', p. 158.

CURRENCY   The euro is legal tender. Coins come in denominations of 1, 5, 10, 20, and 50 cents, and €1 and €2; notes come in denominations of €5, €10, €20, €50, €100, €200, and €500.

DRUGSTORES   Every *farmacia* (drugstore) posts a list of those that are open at night and on Sunday.

ELECTRICITY   The electricity in Sicily varies considerably. It's usually alternating current (AC); the cycle is 50Hz 220V. Check the exact local current at the hotel where you're staying. Getting a transformer is worthwhile if you're carrying any electrical appliances. Plugs have prongs that are round, not flat; therefore, an adapter plug is also needed.

EMBASSIES & CONSULATES   There's a **US Consulate** at Via Vaccarini 1, in Palermo (☎ 091-305857). The nearest **US Embassy** is in Rome, at Via Vittorio Veneto 119A (☎ 06-46741). The **Canadian Embassy** is at Via G. B. de Rossi 27, in Rome (☎ 06-445981). There's a **UK Consulate** at Via Cavour 117, in Palermo (☎ 091-326412), and a **UK Embassy** at Via XX Settembre 80A, in Rome (☎ 06-422-00001). The **Irish Embassy** is at Piazza di Campitelli 3, in Rome (☎ 06-697-9121). For consular queries, call ☎ 06-697-9121. The **Australian Embassy** is at Via Antonio Bosio 15, in Rome (☎ 06-852-721). The **New Zealand**

Embassy is at Via Zara 28, in Rome (☎ 06-441-7171).

EMERGENCIES   For the police, dial **113** or **112**; for an ambulance, **118**; and to report a fire, **115**. For road assistance, dial **116**. For a general crisis, call the *Carabinieri* (army police corps) at **112**.

LANGUAGE   Except in remote backwaters, Italian is the language of the land. (See p. 171 for a brief glossary of useful terms.) English is often understood at attractions such as museums and at most hotels and restaurants catering to foreigners. Even if not all the staff speaks English at a particular establishment, such as a restaurant, sometimes at least one member of the staff does and can aid you. Most islanders also speak a Sicilian dialect. This is a patois comprised of words left over from various conquerors, including Arabic, Greek, French, and Spanish. It's a sort of linguistic amalgam, reflecting centuries of occupation.

LAVATORIES/RESTROOMS   All airport and rail stations have toilets, often requiring a small fee or with attendants who expect to be tipped. Bars, clubs, restaurants, cafés, gas stations, and hotels have facilities as well. Public toilets are also found near many of the major sights. Usually they're designated *WC* (water closet), or *donne* (women) or *uomini* (men). The most confusing designation is *signori* (gentlemen) and *signore* (ladies), so watch that final *i* and *e*! Carry tissues in your pocket or purse—they come in handy.

LEGAL AID   The consulate of your country is the place to turn for legal aid, although offices can't interfere in the Italian legal process. They can, however, inform you of your rights and provide a list of attorneys. You'll have to pay for the attorney out of your pocket—there's no free legal assistance. If you're arrested for a drug offence, all the consulate will do is notify a lawyer about your case and perhaps inform your family. If the problem is serious enough, most nationals will be referred to their embassies or consulates in Rome.

LIQUOR LAWS Wine with meals has been a normal part of family life for hundreds of years in Sicily. Children are exposed to wine at an early age, and consumption of alcohol isn't anything out of the ordinary. There's no legal drinking age for buying or ordering alcohol. Alcohol is sold day and night throughout the year because there's almost no restriction on the sale of wine or liquor in Sicily.

LOST & FOUND Be sure to tell all your credit card companies the minute you discover your wallet has been lost or stolen. Identity theft and fraud are potential complications of losing your wallet, especially if you've lost your driver's license along with your cash and credit cards. Your credit card company or insurer also may require you to file a police report and provide a report number or record of the loss. Most credit card companies have an emergency toll-free number to call if your card is lost or stolen; they may be able to wire you a cash advance immediately or deliver an emergency credit card in a day or two. Visa's emergency number in Italy is ☎ **800-819**; call collect. American Express cardholders should call collect ☎ **06-7220-348.** MasterCard holders should call collect ☎ **800-870-866.** The major credit-reporting bureaus will immediately place a fraud alert on your records, which may protect you against liability for criminal activity. The three major US credit-reporting agencies are **Equifax** (☎ **800/766-0008;** www.equifax.com), **Experian**

(☎ **888/397-3742;** www.experian.com), and **TransUnion** (☎ **800/680-7289;** www.transunion.com). Finally, if you've lost all forms of photo ID, call your airline and explain; they might allow you to board the plane if you have a copy of your passport or birth certificate and a copy of the police report you've filed. If you need emergency cash over the weekend when all banks and American Express offices are closed, you can have money wired to you via **Western Union** (☎ **800/325-6000;** www.westernunion.com).

MAIL Mail delivery in Italy is notoriously bad. Your family and friends back home might receive your postcards in one week, or it could take two (sometimes longer). Postcards, aerogrammes, and letters weighing up to 20 grams sent to the United States and Canada cost €0.80; to the UK, €0.62; and to Australia and New Zealand, €1. You can buy stamps at post offices and *tabacchi*.

NEWSPAPERS & MAGAZINES In major cities, hotels and news kiosks often carry the *International Herald Tribune* and *USA Today,* as well as other English-language newspapers and magazines such as *Time* and *Newsweek*—but they're hard to find elsewhere. There are no English-language magazines or newspapers published in Sicily.

PASSPORTS **For Residents of the United States:** Whether you're applying in person or by mail, you can download passport applications from the US Department of State website at **http://travel.state.gov**. For general information, call the **National Passport Agency** (☎ **202/647-0518**). To find your regional passport office, check the US State Department website or call the **National Passport Information Center** (☎ 877/487-2778).

For Residents of Canada: Passport applications are available at travel agencies throughout Canada or from the central **Passport Office**, Department of Foreign Affairs and International Trade, Ottawa, ON K1A 0G3 (☎ 800/567-6868; www.ppt.gc.ca).

For Residents of the United Kingdom: To pick up an application for a standard 10-year passport (5-year passport for children younger than 16), visit your nearest passport office, major post office, or travel agency; contact the **United Kingdom Passport Service** at ☎ 0870-521-0410; or go to www.ukpa.gov.uk.

For Residents of Ireland: You can apply for a 10-year passport at the **Passport Office,** Setanta Centre, Molesworth Street, Dublin 2 (☎ 01-671-1633; www.irlgov.ie/iveagh). Those younger than 18 and older than 65 must apply for a €12, 3-year passport. You can also apply at 1A South Mall, Cork (☎ 021/494-4700) and at most main post offices.

For Residents of Australia: You can pick up an application from your local post office or any branch of Passports Australia, but you must schedule an interview at the passport office to present your application materials. Call the **Australian Passport Information Service** at ☎ 131-232, or visit www.passports.gov.au.

For Residents of New Zealand: You can pick up a passport application at any New Zealand Passports Office or download it from the website. Call the **Passports Office** (☎ 0800-225-050 in New Zealand, or ☎ 04-474-8100), or go to www.passports.govt.nz.

POLICE Dial ☎ 113, the all-purpose number for police emergency assistance in Italy.

TAXES As a member of the European Union (EU), Italy imposes a **value-added tax** (called IVA in Italy) on most goods and services. The tax that most affects visitors is the one imposed on hotel rates, which ranges from 9% in first- and second-class hotels to 19% in deluxe hotels. When shopping, non-EU citizens are entitled to a **refund of the IVA** if they spend more than €155 at any one store, before tax. To claim your refund, request an invoice from the cashier at the store and take it to the *dogana* (Customs office) at the airport to have it stamped before you leave. *Note:* If you're going to another EU country before flying home, have it stamped at the airport Customs office of the last EU country you'll be in (for example, if you're flying home via the UK, have your Italian invoices stamped in London). Once back home, mail the stamped invoice (keep a photocopy for your records) back to the original vendor within 90 days of the purchase. The vendor will, sooner or later, send you a refund of the tax that you paid at the time of your purchase. Reputable stores view this as a matter of ordinary paperwork and are businesslike about it. Less-honorable stores might lose your dossier. It pays to deal with established vendors on large purchases. You can also request that the refund be credited to the credit card with which you made the purchase; this is usually faster. Many shops are now part of the **'Tax Free for Tourists'** network (look for the sticker in the window). Stores participating in this network issue a check along with your invoice at the time of purchase. After you have the invoice stamped at Customs, you can redeem the check for cash directly at the Tax Free booth in the airport at Palermo or Catania, or mail it back in the envelope provided within 60 days.

TELEPHONES To call Italy from the US, dial the **international prefix**, **011**; then Italy's **country code, 39**; and then the city code (for example, **091** for Palermo or **095** for Catania), which is now built into every number. Then dial the actual **phone number**. A **local phone call** in Italy costs around €0.10. **Public phones** accept coins, precharged phone cards (*scheda* or *carta telefonica*), or both. You can buy a *carta telefonica* at any *tabacchi* shop (most display a sign with a white T on a brown background) in increments of €2.50, €5, and €7.50. To make a call, pick up the receiver and insert €0.10 or your card (break off the corner first). Most phones have a digital display that tells you how much money you've inserted (or how much is left on the card). Dial the number, and don't forget to take the card with you after you hang up.

To call from one city code to another, dial the city code, complete with initial 0, and then dial the number. (Note that numbers in Sicily range from four to eight digits in length. Even when you're calling within the same city, you must dial that city's area code—including the zero. For instance, a Catanian calling another Catanian number must dial 095 before the local number.)

To dial direct internationally, dial **00** and then the country code, the area code, and the number. **Country codes** are as follows: the US and Canada, 1; the UK, 44; Ireland, 353; Australia, 61; New Zealand, 64. Make international calls from a public phone, if possible, because hotels almost invariably charge ridiculously inflated rates for direct

dial. Calls dialed directly are billed on the basis of the call's duration only. A reduced rate is applied Monday to Saturday from 11pm to 8am and all day Sunday. Direct dial calls from the US to Sicily are much cheaper, and so arrange to be called at your hotel if possible. Italy has recently introduced a series of **international phone cards** (*scheda telefonica internazionale*) for calling overseas. They come in increments of 50, 100, 200, and 400 *unita* (units), and they're usually available at *tabacchi* and bars. Each *unita* is worth €0.15 of phone time; it costs 5 *unita* (€0.65) per minute to call within Europe or to the US or Canada, and 12 *unita* (€1.55) per minute to call Australia or New Zealand. You don't insert this card into the phone; merely dial & **1740** and then *2 (star 2) for instructions in English, when prompted.

For free national telephone information (in Italian) in Italy, dial **12**. **For international information**, dial ☎ **176** but be prepared to pay €0.60 a shot. **To make collect or calling-card calls**, drop in €0.10 or insert your card and dial one of the numbers here; an American operator will shortly come on to assist you (because Sicily has yet to discover the joys of the touch-tone phone, you'll have to wait for the operator to come on). The following calling-card numbers work all over Italy: **AT&T**, ☎ 172-1011; **MCI**, ☎ 172-401; and **Sprint**, ☎ 172-1877. To make collect calls to a country besides the US, dial ☎ **170** (free), and practice your Italian in order to relay the number to the Italian operator. Tell him or her that you want it *a carico del destinatario*. Don't count on all Sicilian phones to have touch-tone service. You might not be able to access your voice mail or answering machine from Sicily.

TIME ZONE   Sicily is 6 hours ahead of Eastern Standard Time in the US and one hour ahead of GMT. Daylight saving time goes into effect in Italy each year from the end of March to the end of September.

TIPPING   In hotels, the service charge of 15% to 19% is already added to your bill. In addition, it's customary to tip the chambermaid €0.50 per day, the doorman (for calling a cab) €0.50, and the bellhop or porter €1.50 to €2.50 for carrying bags to your room. The concierge expects about 15% of the bill, as well as tips for extra services performed, which may include help with long-distance calls. In expensive hotels, these amounts are often doubled. In restaurants and cafés, 15% is usually added to your bill to cover most charges. If you're not sure whether this has been done, ask, *'E incluso il servizio?'* (ay een-*cloo*-soh eel sair-*vee*-tsoh?). An additional tip isn't expected, but it's nice to leave an extra couple of euros if you're pleased with the service. Restaurants are required by law to give customers official receipts. Checkroom attendants expect €0.75 and washroom attendants, €0.35. Taxi drivers expect at least 15% of the fare.

WATER   Most Sicilians take mineral water with their meals; however, tap water is safe everywhere, as are public drinking fountains. Unsafe sources will be marked ACQUA NON POTABILE. If tap water comes out cloudy, it's only the calcium or other minerals inherent in a water supply that often comes untreated from fresh springs.

Sicily: **A Brief History**

Coveted for its strategic position in the heart of the Mediterranean and conquered countless times, Sicily has been left with an unparalleled historical legacy. It may be Italian, but Sicilians are Latin by adoption only, volcanic in temperament, and fiercely proud.

From 12,000 BC, the first known inhabitants were Stone Age settlers from the Siculi tribe, originally from Calabria on the mainland and after whom Sicily is named. They were joined by the Elymi, claiming descent from the Trojans and Sicani people from Iberia tribes. Then came the Phoenicians, arriving from Carthage, who settled on the west coast in Solunto and founded Mózia as well as Palermo, establishing important trade routes. By 735 BC, the island was increasingly prosperous and the Greeks began to arrive in search of land for 'Magna Graecia', establishing their first colony at Naxos near today's Taormina. A year later the Corinthians laid the first stones on the island of Ortygia, calling it Syracoussia (Syracuse).

As the Greek colonies grew increasingly powerful in Sicily, tensions mounted especially with the Phoenicians whose colonies were in the west of the island. The Phoenicians' alliance with Carthage (now Tunisia) was also of great concern to the city states of Greece itself. In 480 BC, the Carthaginians were defeated at Himera—and there followed a golden age for Sicily when the largest of the Greek temples was built at Agrigento and classical figures such as Plato, Aeschylus, and Archimedes became household names. Then came the Punic Wars (264–211 BC) when the Romans sacked Syracuse and Sicily was subjected to the yoke of Roman rule until AD 468. Over the centuries the island was used as the Roman Empire's bread basket, as described by the Roman statesman Cato the Elder (234–149 BC): 'the nurse at whose breast the Roman people is fed'. It was not until the 3rd century AD that Sicilians were finally granted the right to citizenship.

After the Romans came the Vandals (of Germanic origins) followed by the Byzantines who ruled from AD 535–827 . In turn they were followed by the Arabs who in 832 conquered Palermo and made it into one of the most cosmopolitan centers in the world. Trade flourished, taxes were reduced, sophisticated irrigation systems built, and an era of religious tolerance began.

The Norman conquest of Sicily took 20 years, but Palermo finally fell in 1071. The Normans made use of Byzantine and Arab artisans and architects in a fusion of talent that was to leave an extraordinarily rich legacy of architecture and art in sights such as Monreale Cathedral and the Palazzo Normanni. There followed rule by the Hohenstaufen (Swabians) whom the Sicilians grew to hate, along with the French Angevins oppressors who imposed high taxes and divided up the baronial fiefs among the French aristocrats. In 1282 the Sicilian Vespers was a popular revolt that killed thousands of the French occupiers and paved the way for a new conqueror, Peter of Aragon.

The Spanish remained in control for five centuries, bringing with them the Spanish Inquisition, decline, and isolation from the Italian mainland. Corrupt nobility ruled and the Inquisition brought religious tolerance to an end. The feudal system forced the peasants off the land breeding frustration in the oppressed population, resulting in the activity of brigands—later known as the 'Mafia'—who found defense from prosecution in a code of silence or Omerta.

During the 17th century, the islanders' misery deepened under continuing misrule. Then came the huge eruption of Mt. Etna in 1669 followed by the earthquake of 1693 and plague and cholera. But, irrepressible as ever, the Sicilians went on to begin a massive rebuilding program, leaving a legacy of spectacular Baroque architecture. Following the death of Charles II of Spain, the Treaty of Utrecht (1713) gifted Sicily to the House of Savoy who then traded Sicily with the Austrians for Sardinia.

In the 18th century the continuing indirect Spanish rule resulted in increased oppression under the privileged and corrupt aristocracy, but with none of the revolutionary spirit of the French revolution. During the Napoleonic Wars the British attempted reform under Lord Bentinck in 1812, who forced the introduction of a two-chamber parliament based on the British model. At this time there was an increase in Malvasia wine production to supply Nelson's fleet that was based in Messina. After the defeat of Napoleon in 1815, Sicily was again under the Bourbons, until the arrival of Garibaldi in Marsala in 1860. On 11th May, he began the Unification of Italy and swiftly swept away the Bourbons. Sicily became free from Spanish rule for the first time since 1282. Yet, once again, the island was in the hands of a distant government and although feudalism was abolished, bailiffs had great power, leasing land from the owners and charging extortionate rents. Local gangs of Mafiosi were used to regulate affairs, and the lack of land reform led to an increasing chasm between the wealthy north of Italy and impoverished southern Italy and Sicily.

In 1908 a huge earthquake in Messina claimed 80,000 lives and this, together with frustration over repression, led to a mass emigration. In 1922 Benito Mussolini became Prime Minister and was determined to suppress the Sicilian Mafia. Thousands of Mafia suspects were imprisoned, thereby pushing the criminals underground. During Mussolini's colonization attempts in North Africa, Sicily was of essential strategic importance. In 1943 the Allies invaded Sicily, pulverizing Messina in particular and a great part of old Palermo and Catania. Amazingly, the Allies were greatly helped by the Mafiosi, who were eager to rid Sicily of the Fascists who had tried to wipe them out under Mussolini. It took just 39 days for the Allies to take Sicily.

In 1946, Sicily became an autonomous region of Italy, and the Mafia helped the ruling classes to suppress communism following the war. In the second half of the 20th century the Christian Democrats political party (with right of center leanings) became the dominant political force working tacitly with the Mafia, on whom they relied for election wins. But the tragic murder of the Mafia-investigating magistrates Paolo Borsellino and Giovanni Falcone in 1992 was a wake-up call to many and has contributed greatly to changing the climate of opinion and finally breaking the Omertà. In 2006, the number one Mafia boss Bernardo Provenzano was arrested after 40 years on the run, followed by his successor Salvatore Lo Piccolo's arrest in 2007. These are important milestones in the fight against the Mafia and there are now many anti-Mafia organizations—'antipizzo'—who have come out publicly to reject the extortion of money—'pizzo'—from shops in Sicily. And yet, as recently as 18th July 2009, reports have come in of the jailing of 49 members (some for up to 20 years) of a Sicilian Mafia syndicate for running protection rackets in Palermo. Official figures suggest that up to 80% of businesses in Palermo pay the protection money to Mafia criminals to continue their commercial activities. But, on an optimistic note, this is the first time that Sicilian business groups, working closely with the police, have achieved a successful prosecution, including the payment of compensation to victims.

Useful Phrases & Menu Terms

Basic Italian Vocabulary & Phrases

ENGLISH	ITALIAN	PRONUNCIATION
Thank you	Grazie	graht-tzee-yey
You're welcome	Prego	prey-go
Please	Per favore	pehr fah-vohr-eh
Yes	Si	see
No	No	noh
Good morning	Buongiorno	bwohn-djor-noh
Good evening	Buona sera	bwohn-ah say-rah
Good night	Buona notte	bwohn-ah noht-tay

ENGLISH	ITALIAN	PRONUNCIATION
How are you?	Come sta?	*koh-may stah*
Very well	Molto bene	*mohl-toh behn-ney*
Goodbye	Arrivederci	*ahr-ree-vah-dehr-chee*
Excuse me (to get attention)	Scusi	*skoo-zee*
Excuse me (to get past someone)	Permesso	*pehr-mehs-soh*
Where is. . . ?	Dovè. . . ?	*doh-vey*
the station	la stazione	*lah stat-tzee-oh-neh*
a hotelun albergo	oon ahl-behr-goh	
a restaurant	un ristorante	*oon reest-ohr-ahnt-eh*
the bathroom	il bagno	*eel bahn-nyoh*
To the right	A destra	*ah dehy-stra*
To the left	A sinistra	*ah see-nees-tra*
Straight ahead	Avanti (or sempre diritto)	*ahv-vahn-tee (sehm-pray dee-reet-toh)*
How much is it?	Quanto costa?	*kwan-toh coh-sta*
The check, please	Il conto, per favore	*eel kon-toh pehr fah-vohr-eh*
What time is it?	Che ore sono?	*kay or-ay soh-noh*
When?	Quando?	*kwan-doh*
Yesterday	Ieri	*ee-yehr-ree*
Today	Oggi	*oh-jee*
Tomorrow	Domani	*doh-mah-nee*
Breakfast	Prima colazione	*pree-mah coh-laht-tzee-ohn-ay*
Lunch	Pranzo	*prahn-zoh*
Dinner	Cena	*chay-nah*
Monday	Lunedì	*loo-nay-dee*
Tuesday	Martedì	*mart-ay-dee*
Wednesday	Mercoledì	*mehr-cohl-ay-dee*
Thursday	Giovedì	*joh-vay-dee*
Friday	Venerdì	*ven-nehr-dee*
Saturday	Sabato	*sah-bah-toh*
Sunday	Domenica	*doh-mehn-nee-kah*

Numbers

NUMBER	ITALIAN	PRONUNCIATION
1	uno	*(oo-noh)*
2	due	*(doo-ay)*
3	tre	*(tray)*
4	quattro	*(kwah-troh)*
5	cinque	*(cheen-kway)*
6	sei	*(say)*
7	sette	*(set-tay)*
8	otto	*(oh-toh)*
9	nove	*(noh-vay)*
10	dieci	*(dee-ay-chee)*
11	undici	*(oon-dee-chee)*
20	venti	*(vehn-tee)*

NUMBER	ITALIAN	PRONUNCIATION
21	ventuno	*(vehn-toon-oh)*
22	venti due	*(vehn-tee doo-ay)*
30	trenta	*(trayn-tah)*
40	quaranta	*(kwah-rahn-tah)*
50	cinquanta	*(cheen-kwan-tah)*
60	sessanta	*(sehs-sahn-tah)*
70	settanta	*(seht-tahn-tah)*
80	ottanta	*(oht-tahn-tah)*
90	novanta	*(noh-vahnt-tah)*
100	cento	*(chen-toh)*
1,000	mille	*(mee-lay)*
5,000	cinque milla	*(cheen-kway mee-lah)*
10,000	dieci milla	*(dee-ay-chee mee*

Sicilian **Cuisine**

What's On The Menu—including Sicilian Specialties

Antipasti Succulent appetizers served at the beginning of a meal (before the pasta). A classic Sicilian antipasto is 'melanzane alla parmigiana' (eggplant (aubergine) baked with parmesan cheese).

Aragosta Lobster.

Arancini Rice balls filled with meat ragù, or with ham and cheese, breaded, and deep-fried.

Bottarga Dried and salted roe of gray mullet or tuna, pressed and cut into slices, dressed with virgin olive oil: known as 'Sicilian caviar'.

Bresaola Air-dried spiced beef.

Bucatini Long, hollow pasta, similar to spaghetti in appearance.

Caciocavallo Firm, stringy cheese, made from cows' milk following a traditional technique that involves hanging the curd over horizontal rods (hence the name, meaning cheese on horseback). It has a smooth, mild salty taste.

Cannoli Crunchy tubular pastry filled with ricotta, candied fruits, pistachios, and chocolate.

Caponata Classic Sicilian dish of eggplants, celery, and other vegetables, as well as capers and raisins, prepared in agrodolce, a sweet-sour sauce.

Cassata The famous Baroque cake of Sicily: sponge and marzipan, filled with ricotta, and decorated with candied fruit.

Costoletta alla siciliana Thinly sliced veal cutlet dredged in bread crumbs, fried, and flavored with Parmesan and chopped garlic.

Falsomagro Beef wrapped around Sicilian sausages or prosciutto, with raisins, pine nuts, grated cheese, and perhaps boiled egg, tied with string and stewed in a savory tomato sauce.

Frittella Simple, seasonal dish made with lightly steamed fresh green vegetables and olive oil.

Gelato (produzione propria) Ice cream (homemade).

Gnocchi Dumplings usually made from potatoes (gnocchi alla patate) or from semolina (gnocchi alla romana), sometimes stuffed with combinations of cheese, spinach, and vegetables.

Granità   Flavored ice, usually with lemon or coffee.

Insalata di frutti di mare   Seafood salad (usually including shrimp and squid) garnished with pickles, lemon, olives, and spices.

Involtini   Thinly sliced beef, veal, or pork, rolled, stuffed, and fried.

Involtini di pesce spada   Grilled roulades of swordfish, covered with bread crumbs and sautéed in olive oil.

Maccù   Soup made from dried fava beans and wild fennel.

Martorana   Marzipan fruits and vegetables.

Musseddu   Traditional Sicilian salted and fried tuna, used to flavor many salads.

Pane con la milza   Spleen and lung sandwich.

Panelle   Chickpea fritters. Pane panelle is Palermo's version of a 'chip butty' (fries in a bread roll).

Pasta alla Norma   (named after Bellini's operatic heroine)—eggplants, tomatoes, basil, and ricotta cheese blended over pasta.

Pasta con le sarde   Bucatini pasta (usually) with a sauce made from sardines flavored with raisins, fennel, and pine nuts.

Pasta coi ricci   Linguini with fresh sea urchin sauce.

Piccata al Marsala   Thin escalope of veal braised in a pungent sauce flavored with Sicilan Marsala wine

Sarde beccafico   Sardine fillets stuffed and rolled with a filling of breadcrumbs, raisins, and pine nuts.

Seppia   Cuttlefish (a kind of squid); its black ink is used for color and flavoring in pasta sauces and risotto dishes

Sfincione Sicilian   Pizza topped with softly stewed onions, tomatoes, anchovies, oregano, and breadcrumbs.

Stiglioli   Lamb or goat intestines, wrapped onto skewers and grilled over charcoal.

Zabaglione/zabaione   Egg yolks whipped into the consistency of a custard, flavored with Marsala, and served warm as a dessert.

Zuppa di cozze   Mussel soup.

Index

Photo **Credits**

Explore over 3,500 destinations.

TOKYO — 7766 miles
LONDON — 3818 miles
TORONTO — 4682 miles
SYDNEY — 5087 miles
NEW YORK — 4947 miles
LOS ANGELES — 2556 miles
HONG KONG — 5638 miles

Frommers.com makes it easy.

Find a destination. ✓ Book a trip. ✓ Get hot travel deals.
Buy a guidebook. ✓ Enter to win vacations. ✓ Listen to podcasts.
Check out the latest travel news. ✓ Share trip photos and memories.
And much more.

Frommers.com